Eckart Meyners

Rider Fitness: Body and Brain

*180 Anytime, Anywhere Exercises to Enhance Range of
Motion, Motor Control, Reaction Time, Flexibility,
Balance, and Muscle Memory*

Translated by Julia Welling

TRAFALGAR SQUARE
North Pomfret, Vermont

First published in 2011 by
Trafalgar Square Books
North Pomfret, Vermont 05053

Printed in China

Originally published in the German language as *Aufwärm-programm für Reiter and Übungs-programm im Sattel* by Franckh-Kosmos Verlags-GmbH & Co. KG, Stuttgart

Library of Congress Cataloging-in-Publication Data

Meyners, Eckart.
 [Aufwarm-Programm fur Reiter and Ubungs-programm im Sattel. English]
 Rider Fitness: Body And Brain—180 Anytime, Anywhere Exercises to Enhance
 Range of Motion, Motor Control, Reaction Time, Flexibility, Balance, and Muscle Memory /
 Eckart Meyners.
  p. cm.
 Includes index.
 Summary: "Step-by-step instructions for rider exercises off and on the horse to better their performance and ability to communicate functionally with their horse"—Provided by publisher.
 ISBN 978-1-57076-482-0
 1. Horses--Health. 2. Horses--Exercise. I. Title.
 SF285.3.M49 2011
 798.23--dc23

                    2011018064

Photos by Horst Streitferdt/Kosmos (all of Part One; pp. 103-104, 110, 113-114, 118, 125 bottom, 132 top, 156-157, 168 in Part Two); Andrea Marquardt/Kosmos (all remaining of Part Two); illustrations by Constanze Keuter
Book design by Erika Gavin
Cover design by RM Didier
Typefaces: Scala, Scala Sans, Strada

10 9 8 7 6 5 4 3 2 1

*This book is dedicated to Heike Kemmer as thanks
for her collaboration.*

Foreword by Heike Kemmer

Protecting the Welfare of the Horse with Good Riding

I am equipped with both natural curiosity and open-mindedness when it comes to anything that could possibly improve my riding and the way I work with horses. So, when I ran into Eckart Meyners at the Equitana Horse Fair in Germany in 2005, I told him that I had heard of his work as a college lecturer on kinetics and riding pedagogy, and I was really interested in having a scientist examine my riding style, seat, and influence on the horse. Right there and then, we made an appointment for a training session, which my horse trainer would also attend.

After only one session with Eckart, I began to notice visible results in my riding. He showed me exercises that improved my ability to relax and follow the horse's movements, as well as control my hands independently from the rest of my body, in an effort to perfect my posture. I was easily able to "become one" with my horse and establish a sustainable form of unity with him. Since that first day, I have had training sessions

Photo 1 *Olympic dressage rider Heike Kemmer with author Eckart Meyners.*

with Eckart once a week, and his exercises have become second nature to me. The things he has taught me about mental training and preparing for competition have helped me tremendously in my efforts to become a better athlete. Therefore, I see it as an honor to have the opportunity to share my thoughts on Eckart's techniques in this book.

It goes without saying that this book is not only directed at competitive riders—it is for anyone who wants to sit more comfortably and perform more clearly and efficiently in the saddle. It will help any rider in any discipline develop a more balanced seat. And ultimately, applying aids correctly (communicating with your horse) is possible only when, as a rider, you are able to move independently from your horse—another important ability honed in the pages ahead.

I once read in a magazine article that the best form of equine welfare is producing riders who know how to sit well—and I can only agree and therefore strongly recommend this book to every rider out there.

Heike Kemmer
*German Olympic Dressage Team Gold Medal Winner,
    2004 and 2008*
Olympic Dressage Individual Bronze Medal Winner, 2008

Introduction by Hannes Müller

The first time I ever saw Eckart Meyners in person was when he spoke at the annual German eventing coaches convention. What he said immediately sparked my interest. What I might describe as almost life-altering, however, was the self-awareness I gained, and which he helps others achieve in all his seminars.

Eckart's exercises stand apart—for example, his "owl exercise" is absolutely amazing: You turn your head, define two points to the left and right of your field of vision, and after a few minutes, you can move in a way that makes you feel like you actually have the mobility of an actual owl (see p. 22). What fascinates me most is the ease and fluidity of his exercises, especially because my earlier efforts to improve my own flexibility and athleticism have always ended in sore muscles or other inconveniences.

I was working as an instructor when I first met Eckart, and facing the difficulty of, on a daily basis, working with motivated students of all ages and levels of training who were finding it very difficult or even impossible to improve bad postures that seemed to hinder the horse in his movements—progress was always minimal. I was able to convince my fellow instructors at the time, Reimund Wille and Axel Stubbendorf, to pay Eckart a visit at his institute in Lüneburg, Northern Germany. This initial "gym lesson" turned into many years of close collaboration and friendship.

When I started working for the Center for Professional Horse Trainers located at the German National Riding School, I immediately began putting in a good word for Eckart and getting him involved in our work. Today, his knowledge and expertise are essential parts of our trainers' professional training. The scientific findings produced when analyzing kinetics are now taught at all levels. Nevertheless, there are still many skeptics who must be convinced of Meyners' methods. I'm happy to say at least 40 of my fellow instructors have gone through additional training to become officially recognized instructors in Meyners' methods, and they are able to offer their students entirely new concepts for instruction.

To me, it is always amazing to see accomplished colleagues with many years of experience and success under their belt change the way their horse moves with a few simple "tricks"— believe it or not, while the horse, warmed up and waiting patiently, watches them do a few easy exercises on the ground.

Eckart's structured approach is his key to success. I am impressed by the energy he puts into his own advancement in his area of expertise, providing us "users" with the latest "tools" when dealing with horses. What he says is always based on the very latest scientific findings. His progressive methods take riding from its traditional past into a functional future.

Without losing focus or turning into a scientist himself, Eckart Meyners always succeeds in organizing his seemingly infinite source of exercises and variations of exercises into his "6-Point Program," making it accessible for all riders. The book you are holding in your hands is taking his approach one step further. By integrating his exercises into actual training situations on horseback, acceptance and application of his scientific work is, in my opinion, spreading and becoming established in today's horse industry.

When my riding students lack the proper physical prerequisites, I have a hard time helping them experience how fascinating riding can be. But by integrating Eckart Meyners' concepts into my lessons, I am able to convey the great pleasure of working with a horse—as a team. Whether you want to or not my dear reader, you too will now have to take a serious look at yourself. With this book, you have found the very latest exercises that have proven extremely useful when you climb in the saddle. You are holding the key to your personal progress as a rider—which, in the end, is in the best interest of your horse!

Hannes Müller
Head of Training, German National Riding School

Part 1

Jp Routines and Workouts on the Ground

t Preparation for Training and Competition

The Importance of a Pre-Riding Warm-Up

Warming up the rider's body in preparation for training or competition is a neglected topic that most people do not think of as important. We pay special attention to warming up and relaxing our horse before a training session, and cool him down afterward (for the most part!), but oddly, unlike other athletes in other sports, we do not see the necessity to include ourselves in this routine.

The fact is, riders who have prepared themselves for training or competition with a proper fitness regime and warm-up can achieve significantly better results in the saddle. As a rider, your physical preparation is a basic requirement for harmonious interactions between you and your horse. With perfectly coordinated movements, you can begin a dialogue between the two of you, and it can be maintained without breaks or interruptions in communication.

In this book we will examine our need to systematically prepare ourselves for riding. We will look at all the issues important to riders. As riding focuses on different aspects of muscle, movement, and coordination than sports like running, soccer, or tennis, certain basic elements of our sport have to be put into perspective. For example, non-riding athletes often push the limits of what is physically possible with regard to speed, strength, and endurance. The only equestrian discipline that might require these kinds of abilities on a regular basis is eventing.

Riding is more of a coordinative sport—that is, it is not about dominating your horse with your strength, but about an easy and harmonious interplay between mind and body of horse and rider. In fact, scientists have found that as soon as you use physical strength to achieve an end, you are no longer able to move either simply or in a gentle manner.

With this in mind, the sport of riding is about:
▸ Elastic muscles.
▸ Mobile joints.
▸ Balance.
▸ Rhythm.
▸ Quick and correct responses to your horse's actions and reactions.
▸ Sensitive differentiation between aids.
▸ The ability to adapt to circumstances.

Photo 2 *Dressage rider Heike Kemmer in a balanced forward seat.*

> ▸ The ability to transfer motion throughout your body.
> ▸ Ideal conditions of psyche.

Riders need to be systematically prepared with regard to their degree of stiffness, lack of suppleness and flexibility, and the extent to which they are able to coordinate the strength they apply, as well as the interplay of all their body parts.

The Rider Warm-Up

Heart Rate and Body Temperature

In order to ensure that the transition between exertion and recovery proceeds as smoothly as possible, the pre-workout or pre-riding warm-up is especially important. You want to activate your entire cardiovascular system. During a proper warm-up, temperatures in your body, muscles, and skin begin to rise. As a result, your metabolism changes. After a period of active riding, sweating will increase the loss of fluids. The sweat evaporates, which cools down the body and decreases the rise in skin and core temperature. Normally, our core temperature runs at about 37°C (98.6°F). In arms and legs, temperatures can be lower by up to 5°C (9°F). The perfect body temperature for riding lies between 38.5 and 39°C (101.3 and 102.2°F).

Respiratory System

During warm-up, your respiration rate and the volume of each breath you take will increase because your muscles need more oxygen to operate while metabolic waste (such as lactic acid) is excreted. Your respiration usually only increases during the first few minutes of a workout. During cardiovascular exercise, you will eventually reach a steady state where your energy intake equals the amount of energy you are expending. Warming up ensures that your breathing rate will already be at "performance level" before your body begins the actual exertion phase (in your case, riding) and leaves you well prepared for the work to come. This is important for your endurance as a rider, such as being able to apply aids over a long period of time.

Minimizing Injuries

The increase in body temperature that a warm-up provides decreases muscle viscosity—that is, internal friction. It also improves the elasticity and flexibility of your muscles, as well as the mobility of your joints. This is important with regard to preventing tension, cramps, and injuries in the rider. Especially when it is cold outside, a higher body temperature lowers the risk of injury to the rider. If your horse spooks and jumps to one side, for example, your muscles need to immediately tense or otherwise become active to keep you in the saddle. If, in a situation like this, your muscles are cold, you might end up with a pulled muscle—or worse.

Photo 3 *Heike demonstrates two easy warm-up exercises: skipping...*

Photo 4 *...and kicking your heels up.*

Improved Coordination and Riding Technique

The decrease in internal friction and increase in flexibility and elasticity of the muscles caused by the rise in your body temperature during a warm-up directly improves the interaction between your nervous system and your muscles. Better coordination (interplay of all muscles) lowers your energy consumption, preventing your body from tiring quickly. You will also be better able to relax active muscles, which has a positive effect on movements that require fine motor skills and a quick succession of aids (such as flying changes and lateral movements, for example).

Nerve receptors in muscles, tendons, and ligaments will become extremely sensitive. The result is a shorter response time for a muscle to react to a nerve impulse and a heightened sense of motion, all of which contributes to more precise interaction with the horse. The rider will experience physical sensations much more quickly. All of these things help the rider adapt to the horse's movements in a more sensitive way and communicate better with him.

Photo 5 *Riding lateral movements requires mobility of the pelvis.*

Joint Capsules, Ligaments, Tendons, and Cartilage

Increased body temperature also plays a central role in preparing connective tissue for use. Only at temperatures between 39 and 40°C (102.2 and 104°F) do the fibers of joint capsules, tendons, ligaments, and cartilage reach their full potential of elasticity and plasticity.

Muscles are able to stretch to an extreme degree (up to 240 percent) while tendons (and ligaments) can only be extended to about 5 percent. And, muscles and tendons take different amounts of time to warm up. Therefore, muscle-tendon units are highly prone to injury.

Joint cartilage receives all its nutrients from synovial fluid, which is produced in the synovial membrane and fills the joint cavity. By preparing for riding with a good warm-up, riders can actually improve the nutritional conditions within their joint cartilage. After a short warm-up, the layer of cartilage becomes denser and after five minutes of moving the joint, the cartilage-nourishing synovial fluid increases. This is especially important to athletic riding performances as the forces produced by the horse are better absorbed, which prevents injuries short- and long-term. Riders stay healthy, longer.

Effects on Your Psyche

Besides preparing you for riding on a physical level, warming up has significant effects on your psyche and leads to emotional stability. Warming up counteracts mental states such as anxiety or inhibition that could negatively affect your riding—that is, it works as kind of an on/off valve for your emotions. This function is especially important with regard to competition, as a good warm-up will prevent you from disturbing your own movements, and those of your horse, with tension, trembling, or nervous actions.

Overall, preparing yourself for riding with a proper warm-up puts you in a state of increased awareness so you are mentally, physically, and emotionally alert—ideal conditions for learning, practicing, training, and competing. It also improves your attitude and increases your overall motivation to work. All of this helps you better adjust to the demands of riding.

Photo 6 *A simple smile or laugh can "loosen" you up, inside and out.*

Controlling Factors in Duration and Intensity of a Warm-Up

Age

Depending on the rider's age, the extent, duration, and intensity of the warm-up phase of their workout—whether on the ground or in the saddle—may vary. The more mature rider has to gently and slowly increase the intensity within her warm-up routines as her body is not as flexible as it once was and is more likely to sustain injuries. In comparison to children and adolescents, the organ functions controlled by the autonomous nervous system in the mature individual adjust to exercise more slowly, which requires the warm-up phase to be longer.

Time of Day

A rider's biorhythm influences the duration of a warm-up. When we sleep, certain body functions slow down or stop altogether, which negatively influences our organs, the elasticity of our muscles, and the mobility of our joints, all of which we feel when we wake up in the morning. It generally takes a while until our performance peaks sometime in the afternoon. Therefore, the time you need to spend warming up decreases during the course of the day since blood circulation and body temperature naturally increase until they reach their maximum at about 3:00 PM.

Outside Temperature

In addition to time of day, climate conditions influence the duration and intensity of your warm-up. High temperatures shorten the duration, rain and cold temperatures extend it. Wearing climate-appropriate clothing helps you cut down on the time you must spend preparing for your workout. Do note, however, that sweating does not substitute for an actual active warm-up.

Attitude

A rider's attitude also plays a role in how long she must warm up prior to working out on the ground or in the saddle. For example, if you consider the riding session ahead to be particularly important, your state of mind will be more alert, and your metabolism will be better prepared to switch from a state of rest to being ready for exercise. A rider's attitude and level of internal "excitement" greatly influence muscle tension and the dilation and constriction of blood vessels.

Physical Fitness

Depending on your current level of physical fitness, you may have to extend or shorten your pre-workout or pre-ride warm-up. As you make a habit of incorporating a warm-up into your daily schedule, you will be able to spend less and less time on it as the overall condition of your nerves, muscles, and joints adapt and improve.

Photos 7–9
Walking or jogging while moving your legs and body in different ways and directions is a fun and easy way to increase your flexibility.

Forms of Warm-Up

General Warm-Up

Goal: Your general warm-up improves your cardiovascular system, increases your body temperature and respiration rate, and prepares your joint capsules, ligaments, tendons, and cartilage for exercise.

A general warm-up targets all the large groups of muscles, even though not all of them are necessarily directly connected to riding. When possible, all muscle groups should be included in your routine in order to improve your overall fitness and condition. This type of warm-up consists of exercises repeated numerous times to stimulate your cardiovascular system and cause your body temperature to slowly rise to its optimum. Work the respective muscle groups, one after the other, and in order to prevent exhaustion.

Photos 10 & 11 *Skipping or hopping improves your overall coordination.*

Rider-Specific Warm-Up

Goal: This type of warm-up is directly connected to riding and decreases muscle viscosity, reduces muscle tension, and prepares for coordinative processes in your body. All of the warm-up routines and workouts featured in this book target one of the six body "areas" of the rider (see p. 15). In addition, you can include routines that focus on improving specific problem areas you might have when in the saddle.

Mental Preparation

The importance of this form of warm-up is generally underestimated. Let's talk about what I call "Observant Training" and "Mental Training."

During Observant Training, you must study the course of a movement in order to improve the mental image you have of it. Incorrect motion patterns develop when your image of a movement (or movement "plan") is incomplete.

Photo 12 *Turning your eyes in the opposite direction from where you are facing improves your "mental flexibility."*

Mental Training is simply playing and replaying the complete movement in your mind without actually observing it (in other words, *visualization*).

Athletes in other sports could not perform without this type of preparation. If an Alpine skier does see the entire downhill course in his mind, and if he has not "gone through" the course via visualization several times before the actual race, accidents are more likely to happen and he is more likely to go off course. Every potential problem area on course needs to be mentally anticipated in order to prevent difficulties with regard to the skier's movements once he is actually out there doing it.

The same principle applies to lugers and bobsledders. On television, you can often observe them closing their eyes right before the start of their race as they mentally experience the entire run once again.

The *ideomotor effect*—when a subject makes motions unconsciously—was first observed by William Benjamin Carpenter, who found that when people see a movement they know how to do performed in front of them, they are not able to dissociate themselves from it, and "emotionally" perform it, too. The external image you observe with your eyes causes you to move along as if you are part of it, internally.

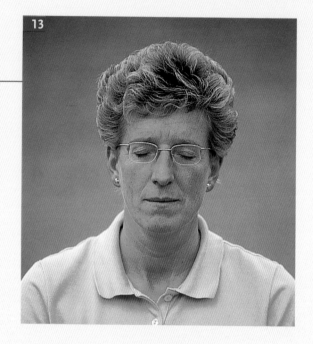

Photo 13 *Mental training (visualization) improves your sense of motion.*

Observing or merely imagining movements you are supposed to perform while riding triggers *ideomotor responses*. This means that biochemically, the same processes take place in your body as if you are riding, even though you are not in the saddle. The prerequisite, however, that ensures this experience is of benefit, is that the rider masters (at least) the basic structure of the movements in question. Once she does, Mental training can be fine-tuned in order to improve the quality of the end result.

Incorrect movements on a horse are always the result of incorrect mental planning. This is why mental preparation is fundamental to good riding.

Active "De-Tiring"— The Cool-Down Process

After extreme physical strain, the body needs to slowly return to its normal state. By performing the cool-down process, mind, body, and soul can regenerate until they have reached the level they normally operate on. This process helps prevent your body from succumbing to negative effects post-exercise or post-competition and leaves it all the more able to perform next time (for more information, see p. 96).

The Basic Structure of the "6-Point Program"

My so-called 6-Point Program was developed upon the request of riding instructors who were looking for a practical series of exercises that would help them help their students quickly change and improve their seat.

The six points of reference in the human body provide a basic structure that your personal training regimen can follow. Their sequence can be changed depending on your specific goals and/or problems. The six points in my program are important connective points or "areas" in your body, which your instructor can focus on in order to improve your seat in no time. (Note: The six points apply to the warm-up and workouts in the saddle in Part Two of this book, too, although they are modified slightly—see p. 121.)

All the individual points are connected to each other in one way or the other. For example, when you massage the atlanto-occipital joint or the base of your skull, you not only experience change in that area of your neck, but you also change the position of your pelvis so that your heels start to absorb your movement, and the horse's, like springs. And, mobilizing the breastbone (sternum) area usually has positive effects on the shoulders so that the subtle rotations riding requires on circles and turns come more naturally to you and you can use the reins more subtly.

POINT 1:
The Head and Neck Area

Your head has superior control over the rest of your body—that is, the head leads and the body follows. Unfortunately, most people do not actually move in this natural way because their head and neck are not positioned correctly. It all starts with the masseters—the thick muscles along your mandible. When you work them too hard, they tense up and restrict the lateral rotation of your head, and believe it or not, even the mobility of your pelvis. The result is you will have a hard time adapting to your horse's movements because your seat is inflexible.

The atlanto-occipital joint and the base of the skull have an even greater influence on your ability to smoothly follow your horse's movements and rotate your body. The atlanto-occipital joint needs to move freely and unrestrictedly. It marks the transition from skull to first cervical vertebra (fig. 1).

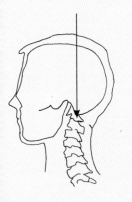

Figure 1
The atlanto-occipital joint.

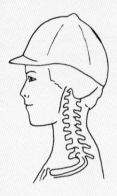

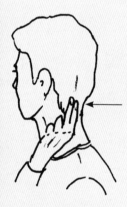

Figure 2 *This illustration shows the rider's neck erect and the focus of the eyes straight ahead and slightly downward. In this position, the atlanto-occipital joint is unrestricted.*

Figure 3 *Several muscle groups originate on the skull.*

Photo 14 *Mobilizing the atlanto-occipital joint relaxes your body.*

If this joint is restricted, all other joints lose their mobility to some degree, and your body will not allow movements to smoothly flow through its entire length. The atlanto-occipital joint can only move freely if your eyes are pointing straight ahead and slightly downward (fig. 2).

In addition, many riders experience negative tension in the muscles around their skull because in their day-to-day existence, they rotate their head in the wrong way (fig. 3). You have to "unlock" the atlanto-occipital joint and reduce the tension around your skull in order to execute rotational movements correctly and completely, and to allow physical sensations and vibrations to pass through your body from head to toe, and vice versa. Taking strain off the atlanto-occipital joint and the muscles that originate at the skull not only relieves your head and neck area, and your upper body, but also allows your pelvis to change position in a way that leads to a more flexible seat and "elastic" ankles.

The basic "seat" of a rider always has to be treated in a holistic manner. Changing your head position can have positive or negative effects on your feet, while in the same way, the position of the stirrups (positioned perpendicular to and under the widest point of your feet) allows your entire body (head to toe) to absorb the horse's movements. If the stirrup is placed too close to the tips of your toes or your heels, all motion transmission within your body is obstructed.

POINT 2:

The Breastbone and Rib Cage

When riding a horse, the vibrations of his movements are meant to flow from your pelvis up to your head, but they are often stopped in the area of your thoracic vertebrae (the middle segment of the vertebral column). This part of the human spine is much less flexible than, for example, the cervical or lumbar vertebrae, as the rib cage acts like a relatively stiff "corset" in that section of the body, allowing for little sensitivity to motion vibrations. For this reason, many riders experience pain in this area when they have to ride at a sitting trot. If a rider has a stiff pelvis on top of this, all her movements in the saddle will be bumpy or jerky. Because the ribs restrict the flexibility of the thoracic vertebrae, you need to pay special attention to mobilizing this area.

POINT 3:

Muscle and Tendon Reflexes

Stress translates into high levels of negative tension in various muscles and tendons. Stretching does not help in this case. However, if you apply what I liken to a "plucking" or "pinching" massage-like touch to (for example) your trapezius muscle in your shoulders and back, pectoralis in your chest, the adductors in your thighs, and the psoas major in your hip, you can loosen the tension and you will feel the difference afterward, especially in the adductor and psoas muscles, which will allow you to sit deeper in the saddle and your pelvis to follow your horse's motion. At first, this "massage" might feel a bit unpleasant, but that only underlines the significance of the muscle tension problem. If you apply it to these muscle groups every day, you will feel significantly better in a very short period of time.

POINT 4:

The Sacroiliac (SI) Joints

Even if all your muscles are evenly developed and work together harmoniously, you will not be able to follow your horse's movements if your sacroiliac (SI) joints (the left and right joints between the sacrum and the ilium in your pelvis) are inhibited or blocked in their movement (fig. 4). Most forms of back problems actually originate in these joints. They are sig-

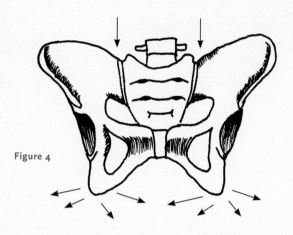

Figure 4

nificant in the human body because they allow for or obstruct our natural motion patterns, which are all three-dimensional (back-forth, left-right, up-down). The sacroiliac joints are indirectly connected to the atlanto-occipital joint.

POINT 5:
The Pelvis

According to the Feldenkrais Method®, the pelvis is, so to speak, the "engine" of the human body, which absorbs and emits energy. The rider uses it to communicate with the horse's back.

Most forms of back problems seen in our society today occur because people do not know how to use their pelvis "flexibly" anymore—this is despite the fact that the pelvis, of all body parts, acts as a "transmission device" that passes on all movements from your legs to your head, and vice versa. It needs to be able to execute three-dimensional movements (see Point 4, p. 17). Stiffness in any one direction will disturb the movement of the horse's back and wreak havoc on the communication between horse and rider.

POINT 6:
The Forward-Driving Aids

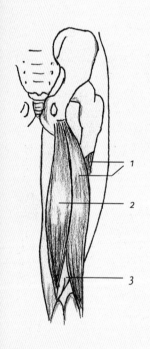

Figure 5

1 *Biceps femoris*

2 *Semitendinosus muscle*

3 *Semimembranosus muscle*

The posterior thigh muscles (fig. 5) are the muscles we need to push our horse forward. The muscles that rotate the thigh bone in the hip joint slightly move the inside of the thigh away from the horse so that—if you imagine a clock face—your left foot points to eleven o'clock and your right to one o'clock, with your horse's head at twelve. Your feet rest in the stirrups at their widest point, and your legs hang down the horse's sides in a relaxed manner. The posterior thigh muscles flex the knees and bring the lower legs close to the horse. These flexors are also responsible for toning (tensing) the lower leg muscles in a natural way that leaves your heels in a deep and flexible position.

Be Creative

The suggested exercises provided in this book include movements that target many different areas of the body. Depending on your interests and needs, you can combine them in any way you like. It is important, however, that you do not do the exercises in a way that targets the same muscle groups over and over again. You do not want to experience fatigue during your warm-up.

General Warm-Up Exercises

- ▸ Jogging, skipping, or heels up (kicking them up to your behind) (photos 3 & 4, p. 7).
- ▸ Moving your limbs in all directions (forward/backward, back/forth/sideways) in order to target as many muscles as possible in different ways (photos 7–9, p. 11).

- ▸ Jumping up and down on one foot or both; cantering like a horse (photos 10 & 11, p. 12).
- ▸ Jumping from left to right while extending your strides (photo 15).
- ▸ Combining skipping forward with rotating your arms gently and slowly forward/backward (photo 16).
- ▸ Skipping combined with rotating your hip area (photo 17).
- ▸ Walking on the balls of your feet, your heels, the outer/inner edges of your feet (photo 18–21).
- ▸ Hopping/jumping in place with a straight/bent upper body, with your torso tipping forward; jumping rope; jumping over ground poles.
- ▸ Conga line (one person leads, others follow, three shuffles and a kick, repeat).
- ▸ Shadow (one person leads and another has to exactly mirror the steps the first person takes—a good exercise when you are warming up as a team).

Riding-Specific Exercises

The exercises presented on the following pages are intended to create perfect energetic, psychological, and coordinative

conditions for riding at peak performance. First, I will intro-
duce you to exercises that optimize your brain functions
while balancing energy between your body "halves" (left/right,
top/bottom, back/front). The exercises improve your cross-
coordination (the ability to work across your body's *midline*—
see p. 136).

Movements that are generally problematic for many indi-
viduals today include rotational motions around the midline,
as well as diagonal patterns. If your body cannot easily rotate
to the side in both directions, you will hardly be able to follow
your horse as he travels on curved lines, such as circles and
turns. Your outside (*outside the bend*) shoulder cannot follow
the movement of the rest of the body—it lags behind and you
will no longer find yourself in the desirable and correct posture where your shoulders are parallel to the horse's, and your
pelvis parallel to his.

Warm-up exercises to train these kinds of coordination
skills have already been introduced in the section on your
general warm-up (skipping and moving sideways while
rotating your hip area, for example). Before moving on with
exercises specific for warming up the rider in particular, it is
important to stimulate the brain and energy meridians (path-
ways), since all muscle functions originate in the brain and
are dependent on energy flow. Therefore, the exercises you
need to do now should not only school your body but more
importantly, your brain.

Kinetic Exercises to Improve Cross-Coordination

Opposite Stretch

Alternate stretching your left arm/right leg with stretching
your right arm/left leg, moving them forward, backward, and
sideways (photo 22). Your eyes should follow your movements
in all directions. Lift your foot to one side behind the opposite leg, and reach back and touch it with your opposite hand.
Switch sides, and repeat multiple times so your hands have
to cross into the lower half of your body on both sides. In
the same way, you can bring your knee up in front of you,
to one side or the other, and grab it with the opposite hand
(photos 23 & 24).

Lazy Eight

Focus on a visual reference point directly in front of you at eye level. This point will be the center of a horizontal figure eight. Stretch one arm out in front of your body in a comfortable manner, and begin "writing" horizontal figure eights in space (fig. 6). You can decide on the height and width of the figure eights, but the best result is achieved if you create one large enough to extend across your entire field of vision and that requires you to use the full mobility of your arm. In order to stimulate the right cerebral hemisphere, start with your left arm pointing at your focal point, and then move it counterclockwise toward the top left half of the eight before moving it in a smooth circular motion back to the center starting point and through to the top right corner of your field of vision and again in a circle back to center. Repeat at least three times and switch arms (photo 25).

You can also do this exercise with your eyes closed. Humming might support the process. Your head (your eyes) should follow the movement to a small degree while your neck remains relaxed.

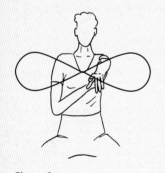

Figure 6

Brain Buttons

I use the term "brain buttons" to describe the soft tissue directly beneath the left and right collarbones (clavicles) and to either side of your breastbone (sternum). In this exercise, place one thumb and forefinger beneath each collarbone and massage these "buttons" vigorously for about 20 to 30 seconds while your other hand touches your belly button (photo 26). Change hands in order to activate both cerebral hemispheres. This exercise might be painful at first, but the sensitivity will vanish after a few days.

You can increase the challenge of this exercise by focusing your eyes in the following sequence (without moving your head): up, down, back to nose level; diagonally from top left to bottom right; diagonally from top right to bottom left; and left to right at nose level. This figure is also called a "butterfly eight."

Balance Buttons

The "balance buttons" are located directly above the indentation where the skull rests upon the neck, approximately one inch to the left and right of your midline (the line that vertically divides your body from head to toe) and directly next to the mastoid process of the temporal bone. Push on or massage the left "button" while touching your belly button with your right hand. Switch hands (photo 27). You can do this exercise standing up, sitting, or lying down.

Space Buttons

Place both hands on your body's midline—one in front, the other in back. Arrange the index and middle fingers of the front hand on your upper lip, while the other hand presses lightly on your tailbone (photo 28). Switch hands to activate both cerebral hemispheres. You can also massage the "buttons" lightly.

Cross-Crawling

Crawl on your hands and knees, then on your elbows and knees, and at lastly, crawl on your stomach (photos 29–31).

Exercises to Reduce Stress

Every rider should "de-stress" before working with her horse, taking a lesson, or competing, in order to mentally prepare to be the best rider possible. I suggest the following techniques, which are easy to follow and create a sound stress-relief foundation to build upon.

Smiling

As a rider, you can positively support your efforts in the saddle simply by smiling (photo 32). When you smile, you activate muscle chains running from your face through your neck area, and your pelvis all the way to your feet. A rider who is smiling will naturally follow the horse's movement with her body.

Positive Thoughts

Besides smiling, pleasant thoughts and feelings improve the suppleness of your seat—only a relaxed rider is able to maintain the balance in her own body and in her horse's. This state of relaxed balance is the prerequisite for sensitive and subtle riding.

Tongue-to-Palate

Due to its stress regulating function, the human tongue plays a special role with regard to the promotion of sensitive riding. When the tip of your tongue is pushed against your palate about one-fifth of an inch behind the incisors, your body's energy is maintained; all energy is "centered."

During riding, you should always pay attention to the tongue's function. It contributes to your balance and should be included in the basic effort of trying to achieve a sensitive seat. Try this exercise to see this phenomenon for yourself: Stand on one leg and ask a friend to gently pull on your arm. You will quickly lose your balance. Do the same experiment this time with your tongue pushing against your palate, and you will be surprised how steadily you are able to stand. Your friend will have to apply a lot more effort to disturb your balance.

Tapping the Breastbone

Your thymus is a specialized organ of the immune system. It is located behind the breastbone (sternum) and in front of the heart. I find that tapping against your breastbone in the area of

the thymus relieves stress (photo 33). Using your knuckles, tap your breastbone a couple of times, several times a day, in order to protect yourself from sources of stress of which you may be unaware. And, in situations that you know to be anxiety producing, this mechanism will allow you to get rid of accumulated stress.

Humming

Human beings constantly experience vibrations throughout their body. When you are stressed, these vibrations are amplified and can make you physically shake. When the vibrations are too low, you behave apathetically and may not act or react in a timely or appropriate manner. When the level of body vibrations is ideal, a balance is struck.

You have probably found yourself in situations—in and out of the saddle—in which you could no longer achieve certain motions you had performed successfully many times in the past, and it may have been due to the level of vibrations in your body (too high or too low). In situations like these, humming can play an important role by reactivating subconscious movement patterns. Humming is also a good way to shield yourself from pressure or criticism—it releases tension rather than bottles it up.

I know of several Grand Prix riders who have incorporated both humming and tapping their breastbone into their basic riding practices with successful results.

Guidelines for Rider Warm-Ups and Workouts

The exercises in this book are intended to sharpen your body awareness, but they must be executed in a certain way to do so. Your goal should be to develop "feel" for your own body, to use movements in targeted and differentiated ways, and to maintain flexibility in all situations. These are basic requirements if you want to be able to apply the many different types of riding aids and communicate with your horse efficiently.

The ideal workout will not only improve your body, it will refine your brain functions, as well (improve the brain's self-organization skills—see Schöllhorn, p. 123). This enables your brain to send impulses of higher quality and variability to individual organs.

This book does not look at muscles individually but instead targets them in groups based on their functions. Repeating the

same exercises over and over again (without variation) might seem to produce physical changes at first, but over time, this kind of workout only maximizes movement in some areas, while restricting it in others—such as speed, strength, or motor skills, including coordination and flexibility. Therefore, the basic principles on how to move your body that follow should always be applied to your riding workout.

Vary Tempo

As a general rule, exercises should be executed in a slow and gentle way. This allows your brain a chance to "see you through them," which improves the quality of your movements. After weeks of slow practice, you can start varying speed and tempo but without repeating the same sequences in succession.

Vary Posture

As a rider, you can develop a feeling for motion and body awareness if you not only practice exercises and repetitions at different tempos but also in different postures. As an example, my basic crawling warmup should not only be practiced on hands and knees (p. 24) but also on knees and elbows and, in the end, flat on your stomach (photos 34–36).

Let Yourself "Be Moved"

It is possible to acquire new motion patterns and to break up established ones. As an example, lie on your back on the floor, lift your legs with your knees bent, and rotate one lower leg in small circles, and left and right, forward and back, from the knee down. Now, do the same thing, but this time take hold

of the leg with your hand and use your hand to move the leg in the same patterns. Your leg and knee will start to trust your hand completely. If you can, ask a friend to move your lower leg for you. Vary the movements in their direction and tempo.

"Being moved" adds new motion patterns to your body's repertoire, which, in this case, makes you more sensitive with regard to correctly using your legs and your pelvis in the saddle. In the exercise just described, your hip joints are mobilized, which will allow your legs to hang down your horses sides in a relaxed manner. Your knees will automatically be lowered and your pelvis better able to follow your horse's movements. (Note: You can also apply this exercise to other body parts, such as your hands and head.)

Switch Sides

Every person has a tendency to execute movements with a preferred limb or on a preferred side of the body. As a result of one side of the body dominating, the difference between your left and right becomes more and more apparent, and coordinating them as a whole seems more and more difficult. All exercises should—whenever possible—be executed with both your left and right side in order to create a muscular balance between the body halves.

In addition, switching sides ensures both hemispheres of the brain learn to work as a team and coordinate your movements (your right hemisphere controls the left side of your body and vice versa). By evenly working out on both sides, you become more sensitive to your entire body, you coordinate your movements in a more holistic and harmonious way, and all motion becomes more efficient.

Vary Muscular Tension

Applying different amounts of muscular strength while completing an exercise helps break up patterns of negative tension. For example, practice an exercises using all you've got (full strength), then repeat applying as little muscle as possible to get the job done. When you vary the amount of strength you apply to an exercise, you will learn to recognize muscle areas that habitually tense up, even when you don't need them. In this way, you will be able to target those areas, relieve tension, and learn to use your muscle strength in a far more efficient manner.

Focus on Balance

Improving your balance automatically heightens all your other senses. There are some exercises you can do on horseback, for example, that go even further to improve your balance (such as the forward seat with uneven stirrup lengths—photo 37). The better your balance, the more sensitive your other senses become. Remember, when doing exercises that work on your balance, you must constantly up the ante—don't let it get too easy.

37

Heighten Specific Senses

Some of the exercises in this book ask you to "turn off" dominant senses (such as sight and hearing) in order to school kinesthesia (a sense mediated by receptors located in your muscles, tendons, and joints, and stimulated by bodily movements). Once you can reduce your dependency on using more dominant senses for physical orientation, you will be better able to listen to your body.

Rider Warm-Up Routines and Workouts on the Ground

Introduction to the Warm-Up Routines and Workouts

Photo 38 *Incorporating a regular warm-up into your day will reduce the time you need to take to prepare your mind and body for a training session, riding lesson, or competition.*

The recommended workouts that follow have been systematically and successfully put into practice by riders at many levels of ability and experience. A long-term commitment to incorporating them in your fitness plan not only trains and sculpts your body, it also helps create new structures and connections in your brain. Ultimately, this cuts down on preparation time prior to a ride, and it speeds up all your coordinated motion patterns during training and competition.

All it often takes to successfully activate new connections from one specific body part to another (resulting in more efficient and/or correct movement) is one simple exercise. "Speed dial" motion patterns (those you can call up and rely on in a moment's notice), however, will only take effect after weeks in which your brain and body have had the time to move through them and adjust to them. (Note that this is also the way to override incorrect motion patterns that may already be engrained in your system.)

The workouts I've provided in this book are composed in a way that allows you to adjust them to your needs. Performing the same workout routine over and over again is bound to get boring. Moreover, the workouts produce different degrees of success, depending on the individual rider—while Rider 1 swears by Workout 1, Rider 2 might feel more prepared after Workout 2 than after Workout 3. You have to find out for yourself how the routines work for you.

Workouts 1 through 3 are based on my 6-Point Program (see p. 15). Workout 4 integrates aspects of strength training in order to help you compensate for and correct muscular imbalances and tension. Workout 5 is based on prenatal and toddler movements—these two early periods in human life are set apart because they are times when we move perfectly naturally and according to our genetics. These early motion patterns are still stored in your subconscious, and by recalling them via related exercises, you can find your way back to a natural state of relaxation and just "being." Workout 6 mobilizes all major joints, while Workout 7 includes axial rotations and left-right movements.

Photo 39 *A proper warm-up prepares both your body and your mind.*

Workout 1

Point 1: Head and Neck Area

Head Shake

Sit on a chair so you can feel your seat bones (ischium). Face straight ahead. Relax your arms and let them hang down by your sides. Using small, quick movements (one-half to one inch only), turn your head very slightly from left to right and back again repeatedly. Instead of tensing up, the muscles in your head and neck should move as effortlessly as possible. Continue the "head shake" for about one minute. Then, turn your head so you are facing to the left, repeat the exercise, and do it again again to the right side (fig. 7).

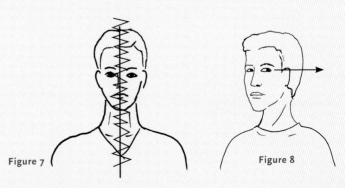

Figure 7   Figure 8

Head and Eyes in Opposite Directions

Perform the same left-to-right head-shaking motion as described above. This time, however, have your eyes move in the opposite direction of your head (fig. 8). Repeat 10 times in both directions. Vary speed of movements.

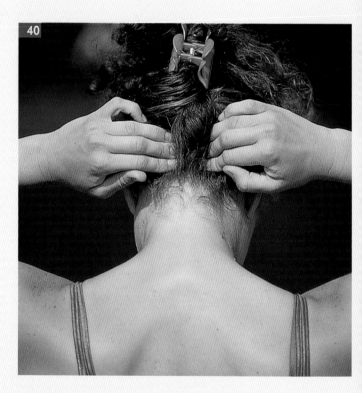

Massage and Stretch the Atlanto-Occipital Joint

It is possible for you to relieve tension in the area around the atlanto-occipital joint (see p. 15) by doing the following massage exercise: With the ring, middle, and index fingers of both hands, massage the point where your skull and uppermost cervical vertebra meet for 10 seconds (photo 40). Follow the massage with this stretching exercise: Place the tip of your left middle finger on your atlanto-occipital joint; place the tip of your right middle finger on your left middle finger. With your elbows stretched sideways, put pressure on the joint. Stretch the area at the same time by slightly moving your head forward and backward (up to a 30-degree angle—fig. 9), again for 10 seconds. Repeat the sequence three times.

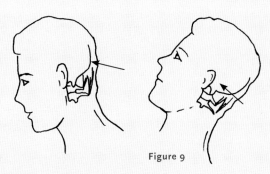

Figure 9

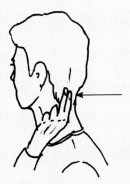

Figure 10

Massage Your Skull

Tension can also be relieved by massaging your skull with your fingers as described above (fig. 10 and photo 41). This area needs to be massaged slowly but intensely as it is very tight in most people due to poor rotational movement of the head. In the beginning, you will probably experience pain, which will fade away quickly if you make a practice of massaging the area several times a day.

Point 2: Breastbone and Rib Cage

Axial Rotation—Focus on Your Hand

Focus on your hand for the entire duration of the following exercise: Stretch your right arm forward at shoulder level, and then bend your elbow at an almost 90-degree angle so your lower arm extends across your upper body and your hand is

about 20 inches from your face. Relax your wrist so your hand hangs down freely. From this position—and while keeping your eyes on your hand—turn your arm as far to the left and right as is possible without straining (photos 42–44). Repeat 10 times and switch arms.

Independent Head Movement

Assume the same pose as in the previous exercise, starting with your right arm. Turn it as far to the left as possible. Hold the pose with your eyes on your hand. Then, turn only your head further to the left before swinging both your arm and head (eyes still on hand) back into the starting position (photos 45–47). Repeat 10 times, then switch arms.

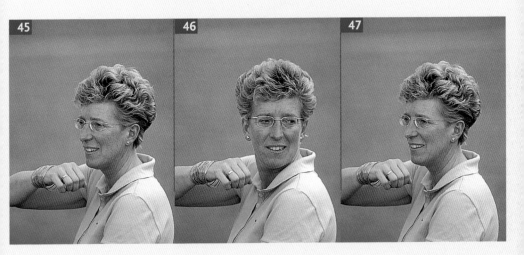

"Eagle"

Lie flat on your stomach, your head resting on your right cheek, your arms stretched out perpendicular to your body at shoulder level. Position your left leg at an angle for more stability. Lift your left arm as high as is possible without straining, and remember the angle you can attain so you can compare with later results. Return your arm to the floor. Now, bend your left wrist upward so your hand leaves the floor, then lift the entire arm with your wrist still bent. Do not lift higher than you can comfortably—you shouldn't require muscle strength or feel like you are working against resistance during this exercise.

Repeat the above sequence 8 to 10 times before turning your head to rest on your left cheek and again repeating another 8 to 10 times with your left arm, which will not be as easy as before. Now switch your leg support: Stretch your left leg and pull up your right one at an angle. Lift your left arm another 8 to 10 times. This movement will be even more difficult (figs. 11 A–D).

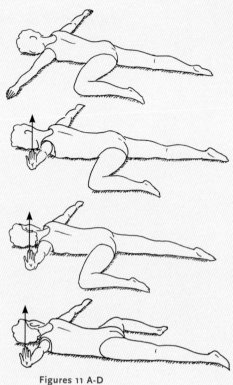

Figures 11 A-D

Finally, turn your head back onto your right cheek and switch legs back to where they started. If you try lifting your left arm again like you did in the beginning, you will find that you can lift it significantly higher now. Repeat the entire sequence with your right arm.

Point 3: Muscle and Tendon Reflexes

Trigger Trapezius and Pectoralis Muscle Reflexes

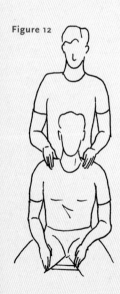

Figure 12

You can trigger the reflex reactions of your trapezius muscle, which extends from the occipital bone to the thoracic vertebrae and to the shoulder blade on each side, by "pinching" or "plucking" at it with your thumb and index/middle finger, preferably when you are lying in bed just after waking up so your shoulders can rest on the mattress and won't have to fight gravity (photo 48). You can also ask a friend to do it for you (fig. 12). The same "pinching" motion, applied along the pectoralis muscle on each side of your chest, can stimulate its reflexes (photo 49).

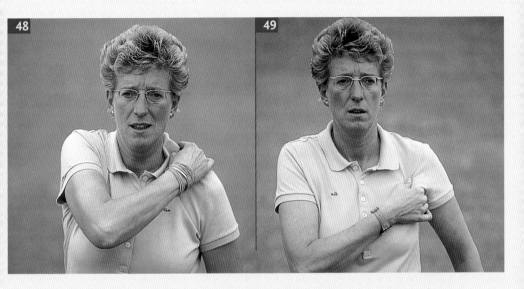

Note: The "pinching" might be relatively unpleasant at first. The feeling of discomfort will fade if you execute the exercise on a daily basis.

Stretching (Relaxing) the Hip Flexors

As with the trapezius and pectoralis muscles, it is possible to effectively "relax" or stretch the hip flexors—the group of skeletal muscles that move your thigh bone (femur)—by triggering major reflex reactions. Relaxing the hip flexors makes it easier for your pelvis to follow your horse's movements; your pelvis will not tilt forward as much as before and will not "lock," becoming more flexible in general.

You can feel your inner hip muscles (a group collectively known as the iliopsoas muscles) when you sit down in a chair and lift one foot off the ground (photo 50). At that moment, these hip flexors tense up. Put your foot back on the floor and rub/massage the muscles from left to right using the tips of your fingers. This may feel very unpleasant, so start gently and slowly increase the pressure. If attended to on a daily basis, these hip flexors will quickly become supple.

The hip flexors along the inside of your thigh, including your adductors, can be relaxed by massaging them as you have other muscles in this book, with a "pinching" or "plucking" motion. Sit on a chair with your legs slightly apart and work your way from your knee up to your pubic bone, using your thumb and index/middle finger to press against the muscle

and "pinch" or "pluck" at it (photo 51). Again, what might feel uncomfortable at first will quickly become more pleasant.

Point 4: Sacroiliac (SI) Joints

Mobilization of the Sacroiliac (SI) Joints

Begin by lying on your back, with one leg stretched out before you and the other bent so your knee is positioned at a 90-degree angle. Move your bent leg sideways over your straight leg and toward the ground—your hand can assist in this stretching motion if it is helpful. Turn your upper body in the opposite direction of your bent leg (photo 52).

Point 5: Pelvis

Face of the Clock

The BALIMO (Balance in Motion) chair has a unique 360-degree swivel seat. It is a valuable tool to help you develop better awareness of and feeling for your body (find out more at www.balimochairs.com). A great way to mobilize your pelvis is to sit on a BALIMO chair and rest your hands on your thighs or let them hang down in a relaxed way on either side of your body. Place your feet shoulder-width apart with your knees either even with or a little lower than your hip joints—never higher. Your body should show four nearly perfect right angles: feet to lower legs, lower legs to thighs, thighs to upper body, upper body to chin.

Imagine yourself sitting on the face of a clock with twelve o'clock in front of you. When you lower your pelvis to the right, you are sitting on three o'clock. When you lower your pelvis to the left, you are sitting on nine o'clock (photos 53 & 54). Change from three o'clock to nine o'clock in two distinct movements, or combine them in one fluid motion. Vary the pace. While doing this exercise, you should be able to touch the ring located underneath the seat of the chair without straining.

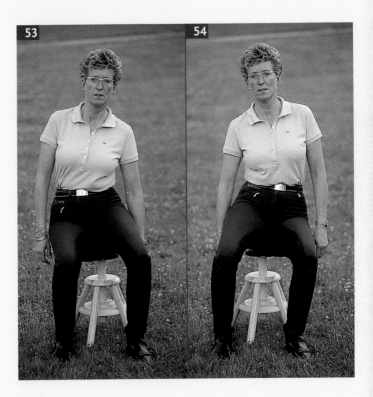

Next, tip your pelvis forward toward twelve o'clock, then backward toward six o'clock. Again, combine in one fluid motion and then vary the pace (photos 55 & 56). Continue with circular motions in all directions (photos 57 & 58). Finally, practice the movements you need to apply lateral weight aids: sit on six o'clock toward ten o'clock or two o'clock (fig. 13 and photos 59 & 60).

Execute these exercises slowly and gently. Even though varying tempo and strength helps your brain learn to adjust and react flexibly to specific movement, you should primarily stick to slow motions in order to improve the quality of your movements.

Figure 13

Point 6: Forward-Driving Aids

Stretching the Muscles Related to the Forward-Driving Aids

Lie on your stomach and stretch your legs slightly apart. Use a small support, such as a rolled up towel, underneath your hips. Alternately, bring your right and left heel up toward your buttocks. Repeat the exercise several times at different speeds (photo 61).

Now stand facing a wall with your arms extended and your hands on the wall. Place one foot in front of the other. Lift your back leg, bending your knee and stretching your leg (fig. 14). Note: Do not bring your lower leg up too fast or you may hollow your back in the process.

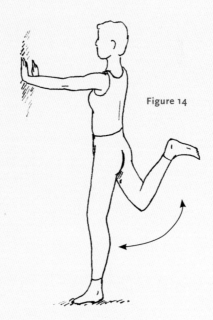

Figure 14

Workout 2

Point 1: Head and Neck Area

Move Your Lower Jaw, Facial Muscles, and Tongue

You can do the following exercises while standing up, sitting, or lying down. Slowly and smoothly, move your lower jaw from left to right as far as possible, while tensing your facial muscles and grimacing on the opposite side (photos 62 & 63). As a variation, move your upper jaw forward and backward.

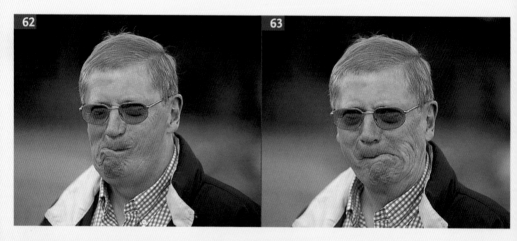

Next, make all kinds of funny faces: Purse your lips, move the corners of your mouth to the outside, and invent other "games" you can play with your facial muscles (photos 64 & 65). Stick out your tongue and point it as far toward your nose,

Figure 15

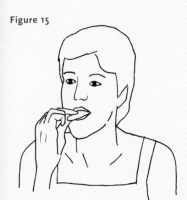

Figure 16

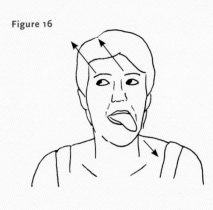

Figure 17

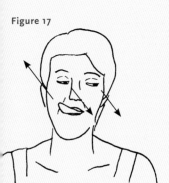

chin, and to the left and right as possible. Then grasp your tongue with your fingers and pull it in the same directions as before—up, down, left, and right. This time your tongue is not allowed to move by itself but must rely on your fingers for direction (fig. 15).

Try coordinating your tongue movements with your eyes. When you point your eyes upward to the left, stretch your tongue downward to the right, and vice versa. When you look down to your left, point your tongue upward to the right; when you look down to your right, point your tongue upward to the left (figs. 16 & 17).

Bounce Your Knees

Stand upright and bend your knees slightly (photo 66). Using your knees to instigate and control movement, move your body up and down. At first, keep your eyes focused straight ahead (parallel to the ground), then lower your nose about 2 inches (not more) and continue "bouncing" your knees (figs. 18 & 19). You will notice changes in the degree of relaxation in your upper body. When your eyes are focused straight ahead, your body will feel more stable than when your eyes are facing downward. If you lower your nose too much in the second part of the exercise, your body will stiffen (as it does when you are riding and look down at your horse's neck).

This is a good exercise to practice on horseback—use short stirrups and train at trot and canter.

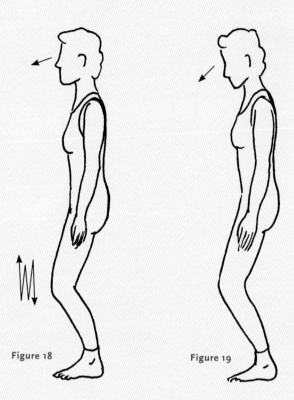

Figure 18   Figure 19

Point 2: Breastbone and Rib Cage

Hand off the Ground

Lie flat on your stomach, point your right elbow out to the right, and rest your right cheek on your right hand. Place your left hand about 4 inches from your nose with your fingers pointing toward your head (fig. 20). Lift your left elbow and make note of how high you are able to lift it. Now, lift your left hand and arm off the ground as high as possible without straining. In a fluid and effortless motion, repeat up to 10 times, and switch sides.

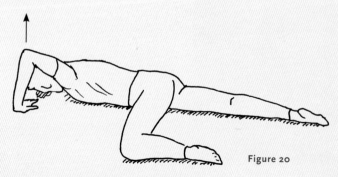

Figure 20

Hug Yourself

Sit in a chair and place your right hand on your left shoulder so that your right elbow lies against your chest. Slide your left hand in between your chest and right arm and place it on your right shoulder. Your right elbow is now resting on your left arm, and your left elbow on your chest (photo 67). With your hands remaining on your shoulders, lift your elbows until they are horizontal and then continue upward, with your eyes following the movement of your elbows (photo 68). The motion should feel pleasant. Do not fight your body when it resists. Repeat the sequence up to 10 times, switch placement of your arms, and repeat another 10 times.

Cross your arms over your chest once again, and lift them until they are horizontal as before. Then rotate your upper body as far to the left and right as possible without straining. Make sure that during the movement, your eyes remain on your elbows. Switch arm positions and repeat (photo 69).

Next cross your arms and lift your elbows until they are as close to perpendicular to the ground as you can go comfortably before turning your upper body to the right and then to the left (photo 70). This should be a smooth motion during which your eyes remain focused on your elbows. Switch arm position and repeat.

Point 3: Muscle and Tendon Reflexes

See Workout 1, p. 38, for exercise descriptions.

Point 4: Sacroiliac (SI) Joints

Kneeling to Sitting

Begin in a kneeling position, and cross one leg in front of the other, then rock back onto your buttocks and into a sitting position (fig. 21 and photo 71). Usually, during a transition from kneeling to sitting, your lower back arches significantly

Figure 21

because you bend your head backward as you move. If you instead tilt your head forward (or in this case, downward), your back will round. Crossing your legs with one knee in front of the other as you transition from kneeling to sitting further emphasizes the necessity of rounding your back during this forward and upward motion. Including the leg crossing—a movement that connects head and pelvis—makes the whole motion easier and more elastic.

71

Point 5: Pelvis

See the BALIMO® chair exercise described in Workout 1 (p. 40). In addition, if you are ready to add new motion patterns to your workout routine, take your pick from the following:

Let Your Pelvis Tell Time

The following exercise should be done in three different positions, one after the other: leaning on your arms, leaning on your elbows, and lying on your back. In all three poses, your legs are pulled up toward your upper body while your knees tip sideways so the soles of your feet touch each other (fig. 22). Imagine a clock underneath your body, and in this position, your pelvis would be located at six o'clock.

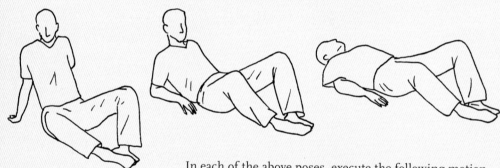

Figure 22

In each of the above poses, execute the following motion sequences, one after the other: Slowly move your pelvis forward so it rests on twelve o'clock (fig. 23). This will automatically hollow your back a bit. Tip your back so it is angled back toward six o'clock. Repeat the motion fluidly several times. (You should be familiar with this motion from the exercise in Workout 1 on the BALIMO chair.) Next move your pelvis from

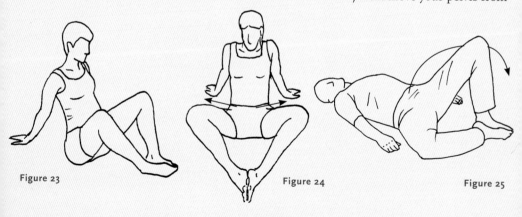

Figure 23   Figure 24   Figure 25

six o'clock toward your left knee, or ten o'clock, and then from six o'clock toward your right knee, or two o'clock (fig. 24). In the end, combine all three movements in one fluid motion: six to ten, six to twelve, six to two, and back again.

Active and Reactive Knee Movement

Lie on your back and pull your knees toward you so the soles of your feet rest flat on the ground. Move your knees from left to right toward the floor—move one knee actively while allowing the other to follow reactively (fig. 25). Alternatives include asking a friend to move your knees for you, or moving both knees actively while maintaining a distance of about 4 inches between them. Try all versions, then alternate.

Point 6: Forward-Driving Aids

Conscious Driving Motions (Resistance Training)

Lie on your stomach with a small source of support under your hips, such as a rolled up towel, and stretch your legs slightly apart. Alternately lift your right and left heels toward your buttocks. Ask a friend to hold on to you lower legs in order to add resistance. Your assistant should vary the resistance so your flexor muscles become more sensitive and you learn to apply your driving aids with more or less strength, as necessary, and at different speeds (photo 72).

72

As an alternative, your assistant can use a resistance band or a sturdy bicycle tube to increase the challenge (photo 73). Lie down in the same position as described above. Your friend should wrap the resistance band around your ankle and either hold one end or tie it to an immovable object. Again, lift your heel in the direction of your buttocks. You can increase the resistance and the amount of strength you have to apply by sliding away from your friend or the object. Switch legs and repeat.

Workout 3

Point 1: Head and Neck Area

Your Head as a Wheel

Go down on all fours in a crawling position and rest your head on the floor with your forehead touching the ground. Slowly roll your head toward your nose so the back of your neck and upper back curve down toward the ground, then roll your head back to starting position so it is again resting on your forehead (figs. 26 A & B).

You can vary this exercise by changing the position of your knees. Put one knee about 6 inches in front of the other and perform the same rolling motion with your head (photo 74).

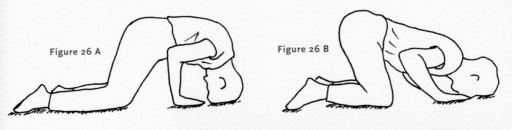

Figure 26 A   Figure 26 B

Switch knee positions. An observer should be able to see how the movement is transferred from your left hip to your right shoulder, and right hip to your left shoulder, respectively (figs. 27 A & B).

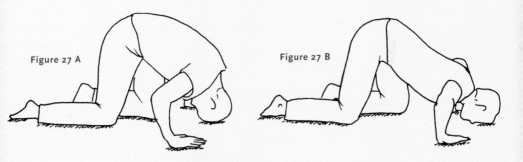

Figure 27 A   Figure 27 B

Head Side-to-Side

Sit down on the right side of a chair on your left buttock only, leaving your right buttock freely suspended. Place your left foot in front of you while the right one supports you from underneath your center of gravity. Place your right hand on your head. In this exercise your hand should control your head's movement, slowly moving your head from left to right—only as far as possible without straining or causing pain (fig. 28).

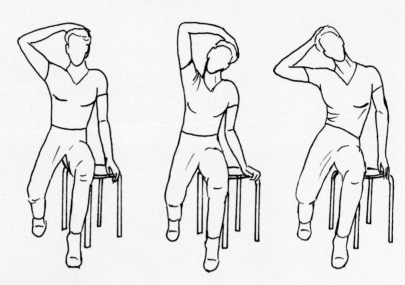

Figure 28

75

Do not attempt to "work through" resistance. When your head is moved, your suspended buttock will lower below the level of the seat and lift in the direction of your shoulder.

Repeat 10 times, then switch sides: With your right buttock, sit on the left side of the chair. Slide your right foot forward and your left one back underneath your center of gravity. Place your left hand on your head and move the latter gently from left to right (photo 75).

Point 2: Breastbone and Rib Cage

Use Your Hands to Crawl

Lie on the floor, face down, and push your palms onto the floor to elevate your upper body and prepare to pull your body forward with one hand and then the other (fig. 29). Pushing your palms onto the floor bends your wrists, which stretches the muscles in your elbows, arches your shoulders, and twists your spine. Your breastbone is mobilized and your arms take on their original function as "forelegs." This leads to an increase in the quality of your upper body movements.

Your Arm Leads Your Upper Body

Lie on your side with a pillow supporting your head. Bend both arms at a right angle and place your palms against each other. Pull your knees up so your thighs are perpendicular to your upper body. Move your top leg slightly so your top knee lies on the floor in front of bottom knee (fig. 30 A).

Figure 29

Lift your upper arm until it is vertical and then lower it to starting position (fig. 30 B). Repeat 10 times. As a variation, focus your eyes on your hand while lifting your arm. Repeat 10 times more. Next, lift your upper arm beyond the vertical, but make sure your top knee remains on the floor. Then, as in the previous exercise, repeat while keeping your eyes focused on your hand.

Finally, lift your arm even further (this time, your knee may leave the floor). Repeat with your eyes focused on your hand. Keep practicing until your upper arm touches the ground behind your back (fig. 30 C). Hold this pose for several seconds before repeating the entire sequence on the other side.

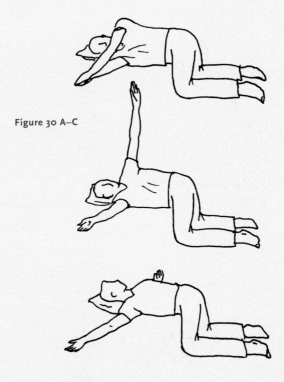

Figure 30 A–C

Point 3: Muscle and Tendon Reflexes

See Workout 1 (p. 38) for exercises.

Point 4: Sacroiliac (SI) Joints

Twist Your Body

Lie on your back and pull your legs toward you until the soles of your feet are flat on the ground. Place your right ankle on your left knee and move your legs smoothly from left to right toward the floor (fig. 31 A). Move as far to each side as possible. This should be one continuous motion—do not stop when you cannot go any further one way, but instead immediately start moving your legs back the other way. Vary your pace: While the general speed of your movements should be slow, you are allowed to accelerate your movements several times. Repeat with your left ankle on your right knee.

Repeat the above steps with a rolled-up yoga mat underneath your buttocks (fig. 31 B). Then move the mat underneath your lumbar spine. By varying the position of the mat, you increase the mobilizing effect on your sacroiliac (SI) joints.

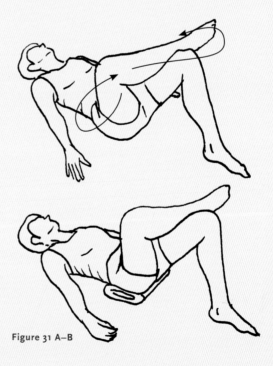

Figure 31 A–B

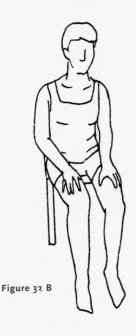

Figure 32 A   Figure 32 B   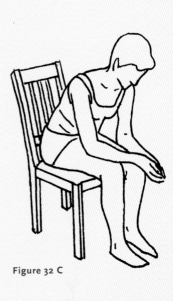

Figure 32 C

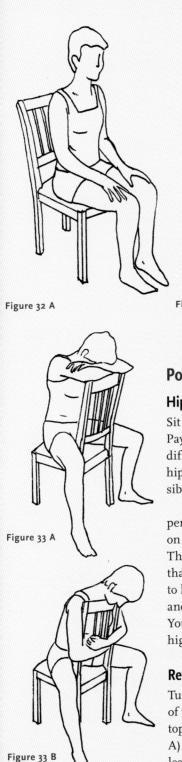

Figure 33 A

Figure 33 B

Point 5: Pelvis

Hip movements on a chair

Sit on a chair and alternate lifting your left hip and your right. Pay attention to how high you are able to lift each hip and how difficult it is for you. Repeat the movement 10 times with each hip. Then, sit as far forward on the edge of the chair as possible and again repeat 10 times (figs. 32 A & B).

Slide all the way back toward the backrest and lean your upper body forward. Support yourself with your forearms placed on your thighs (fig. 32 C). Lift each hip another 10 times. Then, shift all your weight to one forearm so your weight on that thigh "blocks" movement in the respective hip joint. Try to lift that hip 10 times. Shift your weight to the other thigh and repeat. Finally, repeat the very first part of the exercise. You will notice that you are able to lift your hips significantly higher and that the movement feels much easier.

Reverse Hip Movements on a Chair

Turn a chair around and straddle it with the backrest in front of you. Place your forearms one on top of the other along the top of the backrest, and rest your forehead on them (fig. 33 A). As with the last exercise, lift each hip 10 times. Then, lean your chest against the backrest and "hug" the backrest with your arms (fig. 33 B). Repeat the hip movements, which you will find rather difficult this time. Finally, return to the forward-facing position from the last exercise, with your back against the backrest, and repeat the hip movements. How easy or difficult have they have become? How high you can you now lift your hips?

Hip Movement on a Clock Face

Sit on a chair and imagine a clock face on the seat's surface. Move your pelvis forward and back on the clock face, from six to twelve o'clock (figs. 34 A & B). Pay attention to how this movement feels to you. Now, execute all steps from the first two exercises for the pelvis while continuing with the six-to-twelve clock movement. Check your pelvis mobility after the exercise—you will find that it has increased and moving your hips is easier.

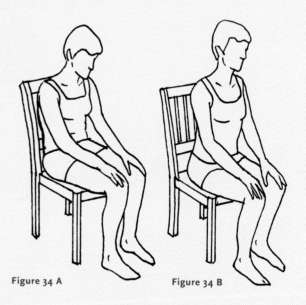

Figure 34 A   Figure 34 B

Point 6: Forward-Driving Aids

Strengthen the Muscles that Drive Your Horse Forward

Begin in a reverse plank pose on your feet and elbows. Stretch your hips upward so your legs and upper body form one straight line (fig. 35). Hold for 10 or more seconds, depending on your level of fitness. Repeat at least three times.

Figure 35

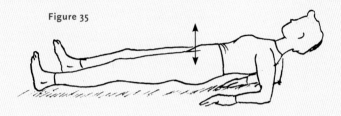

Now lie on your back, bend your hips and knees at a right angle, and rest your heels on the seat of a chair. Lift your buttocks as far off the ground as possible (fig. 36). Hold for 10 or more seconds, depending on your level of fitness. Repeat at least three times.

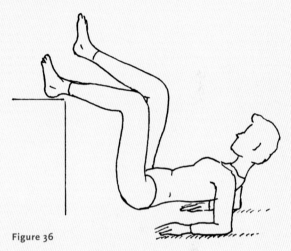

Figure 36

Dynamic Stretching

Begin standing upright, facing a chair. Rest one heel on the chair seat and cross your arms behind your back. Pull the tips of your toes toward you as far as possible while leaning your upper body and pelvis forward (fig. 37). Slowly and gently, swing forward several times.

Note: Do not collapse your hip or round your back! Keep your knees slightly bent—do not hyperextend them. You may support yourself if you lose your balance.

Next, lie on your back, close your hands around one thigh just above the knee, and pull your knee toward your chest while stretching the other leg out before you (fig. 38). Pull up the tips of your toes on both feet. Repeat stretching your lower leg and pulling up your toes several times. Note: The thigh

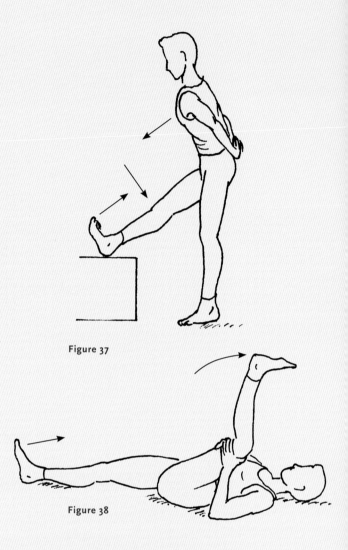

Figure 37

Figure 38

you pull toward your chest must remain on your chest during the entire exercise.

In the workouts that follow, we will no longer stick to the structure of my 6-Point Program, but instead continue with routines that target other important aspects of fitness training. To be specific, we will focus on: strength training as a basis of warm-up; mobilization of all major joints to holistically improve transfer and flow of motion throughout the body; rediscovery of natural motion patterns via execution of movements characteristic of the prenatal and toddler phase of life; and axial rotation to improve your seat and to sensitize your left-right and cross-coordination.

Workout 4: Strength Training to Correct Muscular Imbalance and Improve Suppleness

Basic Guidelines for Workout 4

This workout includes two stretching exercises, followed by specific exercises to strengthen your muscles—both flexors and extensors. Experience has shown that, after completing Workout 4, riders feel as relaxed, flexible, and coordinated as they do after completing Workouts 1–3 (pp. 33–60). We advise you to do this routine in addition to the others in order to increase muscle mass and to get better overall fitness results.

When you stretch, move slowly and dynamically. During a warm-up, stretching statically can decrease muscle strength (up to 20 percent) and reduce stability in your muscles.

When your goal is to stretch your muscles, slowly move into the end position during each repetition and hold for 10 seconds. Depending on your level of fitness, you can hold for 15, 20, or 30 seconds. Rest for 10 seconds before repeating two more times. Repeat the stretch on the opposite side.

The same principle applies to the strengthening exercises that follow the stretches. Repeat each of them 10 times (on each side, when applicable). It is possible to combine static and dynamic motion sequences.

Head and Neck Area

Stretching the Neck/Back of the Neck Muscles

Note: Always be very careful when stretching this area.

POSITION 1:
Lie flat on your back, pull your legs toward you and fold your hands behind your head. Lift your head and with your hands, and pull forward-and-upward (fig. 39 and photo 76).

Figure 39

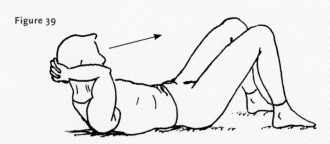

Position 2:

Stand with your legs shoulder-width apart. With your right hand, pull your head as far to the right as possible while pushing your left arm toward the floor (fig. 40 and photo 77). Switch sides and repeat.

Position 3:

Stand with your legs shoulder-width apart. With your right hand, pull your head forward-and-sideways (fig. 41 and photo 78).

Position 4:

Stand with your legs shoulder-width apart. Stretch one arm out in front of you at neck level, then bend at your elbow so your lower arm crosses in front of you. With the hand of your other arm, push your elbow toward your neck (fig. 42).

Upper Body

Vertical Abdominals/Back Muscles

Exercise 1:

Lie on your back and rest your lower legs on a chair seat, bend-

Figure 40

Figure 41

Figure 42

ing your knees and hips at a right angle. Cross your arms in front of your upper body. Slowly lift your upper body, but do not pull your head toward your chest while doing so (fig. 43 and photo 79)

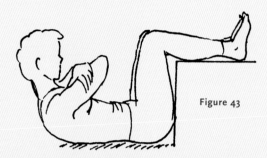

Figure 43

79

Exercise 2:

Roll up a towel or blanket. Lie on your stomach with the towel underneath your pelvis. Fold your hands behind your head and slightly lift your upper body off the floor. Do not tilt your head backward; keep your eyes on the floor (fig. 44).

Exercise 3:

Lie on your back and again rest your lower legs on a chair, bending your knees and hips at a right angle. Stretch your arms out in front of you. Slowly lift your upper body, moving your hands in the direction of the chair (fig. 45 A & B).

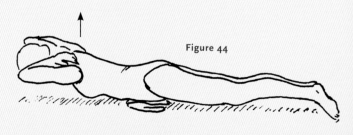

Figure 44

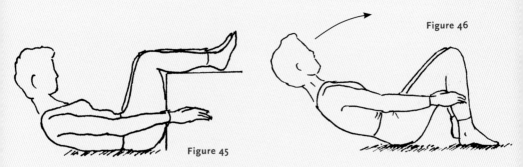

Figure 46

Figure 45

EXERCISE 4:
Roll up a towel or blanket. Lie on your stomach with the towel underneath your pelvis. Fold your hands behind your head and lift your legs off the floor, tensing up your gluteal muscles.

EXERCISE 5:
Lie on your back, pull your legs toward you and stretch your arms forward. Slowly lift your upper body off the floor and stretch your arms past your legs (fig. 46).

EXERCISE 6:
Kneel down with your upper body in a "bowed" position toward the floor, and cross your arms behind your head. Lift your upper body and stretch your spine (fig. 47 A & B).

Figure 47 A

Figure 47 B

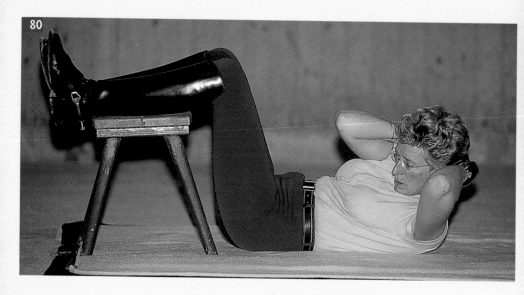

Oblique Abdominals/Diagonal Movements for Your Back Muscles

EXERCISE 1:

Lie on your back, bend your knees and hips at a right angle, with your lower legs in the air (or, if necessary, use a chair to support them). With your hands behind your head or your hands joined in a fist out in front of you, stretch your upper body and lift one shoulder diagonally off the floor toward your opposite leg. When your hands are joined in front of you, they should move past the outside of your thigh (fig. 48 and photo 80).

Figure 48

EXERCISE 2:

Start on your hands and knees. Alternate lifting your right arm and left leg out ahead and behind you, respectively, then pulling your right elbow and left knee underneath your body (figs. 49 A & B). Switch sides and repeat. Note: Do not lift your arms and legs above shoulder level in order to prevent hollowing your back.

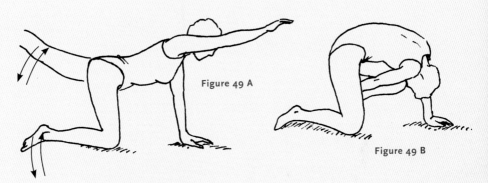

Figure 49 A

Figure 49 B

EXERCISE 3:

Lie on your back, stretch your arms out to the sides, and bend your knees and hips at a right angle with your legs slightly apart. Move your legs to each side until they touch the ground (figs. 50 A & B).

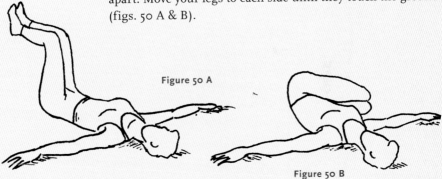

Figure 50 A

Figure 50 B

EXERCISE 4:

Roll up a towel or blanket. Lie on your stomach with the towel underneath your pelvis. Fold your hands behind your head and slightly lift your upper body off the ground without tilting your head backward as in Exercise 2 on p. 64. However, this time keep your eyes focused on the floor while alternating turning your shoulder girdle until the opposite elbow touches the floor (figs. 51 A & B).

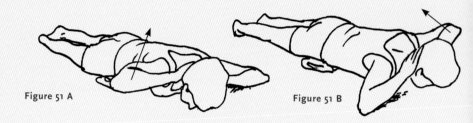

Figure 51 A   Figure 51 B

Front and Back of Your Body

EXERCISE 1:

Assume a reverse plank pose, supporting yourself on your
forearms. Lift your buttocks by stretching your hip joints upward. You want your upper body and legs to form one straight
line (fig. 52).

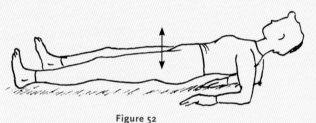

Figure 52

EXERCISE 2:

Lie flat on your stomach, your forearms on the floor. Slowly
lift your buttocks so your body weight rests on your forearms
and tips of your toes in a plank pose (fig. 53). Stretch your body
so it forms one straight line from head to heels. Do not bend in
your pelvic area.

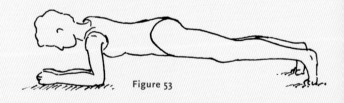

Figure 53

EXERCISE 3:

Assume the reverse plank position as in Exercise 1. Lift one
leg until the front of your body is aligned in one straight line
(fig. 54). This will work the buttocks. Switch legs.

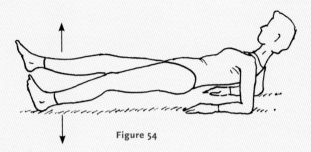

Figure 54

EXERCISE 4:

Begin in the plank position described in Exercise 2. This time, lift one leg at a time as in Exercise 3, flexing your buttocks (fig. 55).

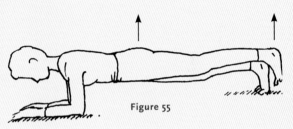

Figure 55

Left and Right Sides of Your Body

Execute all exercises first with your right side and then with your left.

EXERCISE 1:

Assume a side plank pose with your weight resting on one arm and supporting yourself with your free hand on the floor in front of your body. Lift your pelvis until the upper side of your body becomes one straight line (fig. 56). Note: Do not collapse your hip. Your entire body must be part of the stretch (torso—front and back). Switch sides.

Figure 56

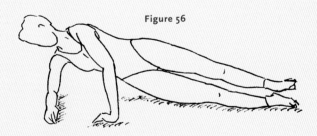

EXERCISE 2:

Assume the side plank pose with your weight resting on one arm—this time without using your free hand for additional support. Lift your pelvis until the upper side of your body becomes one straight line (fig. 57). Note: As before, do not collapse your hip. Switch sides.

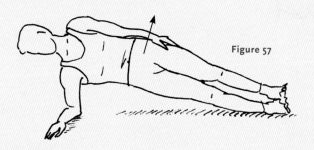

Figure 57

EXERCISE 3:

Assume the side plank pose as in Exercise 2. Again lift your pelvis and once your body is stretched in one straight line, lift your upper leg (fig. 58).

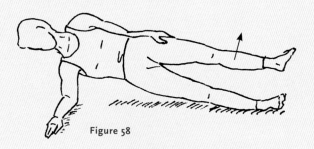

Figure 58

EXERCISE 4:

Lie on your side, your body completely stretched out, from your fingers to your feet. Lift both legs off the ground, slightly apart (fig. 59).

Figure 59

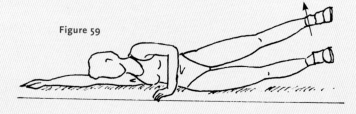

Whole Body Stretch—Back and Front

EXERCISE 1:
Roll up a towel or blanket. Lie on your stomach with the towel underneath your pelvis. Stretch your arms out in front of you. Simultaneously, lift your upper body and legs off the ground so your body forms one straight, balanced line (fig. 60). Note: Avoid hollowing your back.

Figure 60

EXERCISE 2:
Lie on your back with your rolled up towel or blanket underneath your buttocks. Stretch your arms out beside your body. Simultaneously lift your upper body and legs off the ground so your body becomes one straight, balanced line (fig. 61).

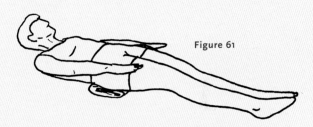

Figure 61

Workout 5: Regain Natural Movements Using Fundamental Motion Patterns

The following workout, inspired by my work with the Brain Gym® (see p. 128), introduces you to exercises based on basic patterns of movement typical for the prenatal and toddler phases of our life—a period of time during which we still move naturally and as genetically designed. These motion patterns are stored in our subconscious, which makes it relatively easy to reactivate them. By doing so, you will be able to develop perfect riding posture without having to execute complicated motion sequences.

The exercises that follow come with many variations and should be done in a way that is easy and playful: You will be changing directions, poses, pace, and level of effort (strength). Variation helps interrupt persistent false motion patterns or negative tension in your body.

After performing this workout, riders reported their movements felt easy, fluid, and relaxed. Only a relaxed muscle can be used accurately and with all its elasticity. The slightest tension is enough to disturb your coordination and prevent you from following and influencing your horse's movements as you desire.

All of the following exercises improve cross-coordination and the rotation of your upper body, which is important when riding. (For example, one shoulder and one side of your pelvis move in opposite directions when you turn your horse.)

Freestyle Walking/Jogging

Walk or jog at different paces, and in different directions—forward, backward, and sideways. Do not take more than five or six steps in the same direction. By mixing up speed and direction, all muscles involved in the movements are exercised. Since walking and jogging require left-right coordination, the exercise reactivates motion patterns you used to apply when you were very young (fig. 62).

Figure 62

Step Ups

Stand next to a sturdy crate, step-up platform, or even a
ground pole, and place one foot on top of it. Stretch upward
until you are standing on top of the crate or platform on one
foot. Make sure that when you stretch the leg, your entire
body stretches too: Move your hips forward and straighten
your upper body (figs. 63 A & B). Imagine a screw winding
its way straight down through your body as you do so. Repeat
with the other leg.

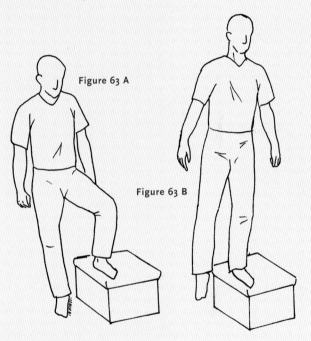

Figure 63 A

Figure 63 B

Rocking and Rolling

EXERCISE 1:

Begin this series moving left to right. Lying flat on your back,
pull your knees toward your body, grab your left knee with
your left hand and your right knee with your right hand. Rock
slowly from left to right, at first very subtly and increasing the
movements until the backs of your hands touch the floor on
either side (photos 81–84). The motion should be slow, gentle,
and fluid. Mix up the pace and change the amount of space
between your thighs.

Exercise 2:

Begin as you did in Exercise 1, but this time gently rock backward and forward. Your movements should be minimal at first before slowly increasing their scope until you roll all the way forward into a sitting position (fig. 64) and all the way backward with your knees almost touching the ground on either side of your head. Vary the pace, the space between your thighs, and also the distance between your legs and your upper body.

Figure 64

EXERCISE 3:

If you have trouble executing Exercise 2, you can adapt it to
your needs: Grab one knee with both hands and use your
other outstretched leg to gain momentum. This will make it
easier to roll forward into a sitting position (figs. 65 A & B).
After performing the forward-and-back roll this way several
times, try again as described in Exercise 2 in order to feel the
difference between moving with a straight back and moving
with a rounded one.

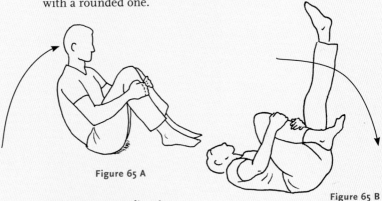

Figure 65 A

Figure 65 B

Improving Coordination

EXERCISE 1:

Lie flat on your stomach, support yourself with your hands
on either side, and pull one knee forward to one side of your
body. Working against the resistance of the floor mobilizes the
hip on that side (figs. 66 A & B). Pull the other knee forward.
Crawling forward like this on your stomach makes your spine
aware of how to move in order to put your feet in the right
position to walk. After this exercise, your body will be able to
"absorb" your steps and gently push itself off the ground. You
can also do this exercise supporting yourself on your forearms
instead of on your hands.

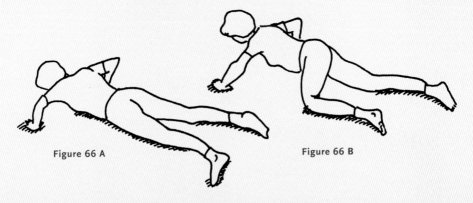

Figure 66 A

Figure 66 B

EXERCISE 2:

It is difficult to move your head toward your shoulder. People often experience negative tension in various parts of their body when they try. My solution is to not only move your head toward your shoulder but to also move your shoulder toward your head at the same time. Try this to one side and then the other—sit with your knees apart and your feet together, and first move your head toward your shoulder, noting when you begin to feel resistance. Now try bringing your head to one shoulder, while at the same time bringing that shoulder to your head (fig. 67). By reinstalling this unity, your entire body will rediscover its natural motion patterns, and once your head and shoulders have gotten used to approaching each other, the movements of your head will become freer in general.

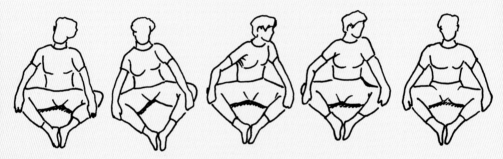

Figure 67

You can turn this simple exercise into a rolling movement where you roll onto your side, then your back, your other side, and back up into a sitting position. Reach down and grab your ankles, with your elbows against the inside of your thighs. It is important that you keep your hands around your ankles and your elbows close to your thighs during the exercise; your upper body and legs need to become one closed system during the rolling motion. In the beginning, it might be difficult to get back up into a sitting position once you have rolled onto your side (photos 85–89).

EXERCISE 3:

In this exercise, you will effectively "walk on your shoulders." Lie on your back and bend your knees so your feet are flat on the floor. Stretch your pelvis upward so your buttocks are raised off the ground and "walk" taking alternating steps with your shoulders (fig. 68 and photo 90). The movement of your

pelvis will relax the muscles in your shoulder blades, and the stiff upper section of your back that remains pressed against the floor will be loosened up by its integration in the movement as a whole. The mobility in your shoulders and arms will also increase.

Figure 68

Workout 6: Mobilizing Major Joints

Transmission of motion from your pelvis to your head or feet is possible only if none of the major joints (ankles, knees, hips, shoulders, wrists, and atlanto-occipital joint) obstruct the flow of motion. By mobilizing these joints, it is easier for body parts—and their simultaneous or successive movements—to connect to each other. Ankle flexibility, for example, can be achieved various ways, but is mostly dependent on the mobility of your hip joints. And believe it or not, mobilizing your atlanto-occipital joint (see p. 15) also leads to elastic ankles.

If some areas of your body are relaxed (mobile) while others are stiff, your body will resort to countermovements (movements made in opposition to others), which have significant negative effects on your horse. This is why you need to "loosen up" in general so all movements feel easy and can flow through your entire body at all times. This allows you to develop a secure, stable (but not stiff!) posture, while at the same time coordinating your movements. The following, specialized workout will help you in your efforts to achieve these goals.

Head and Neck Area

Execute the following movements in a slow and gentle manner: Roll your head forward and pause for a short moment before gently rolling your head left and right. Tilt your head backward before gently tilting it from left to right once again (photos 91– 93). (Note: Be sure you are not moving your head in a circle, but in four distinct directions.) Breathe rhythmically during the entire exercise and do not go push your head to the "end" position in any direction, as this leads to negative tension.

While tilting your head backward, keep your mouth slightly open. You need to always be able to swallow. If you find a "knot" in a muscle, hold the pose for a while until the tension has subsided. Relax your shoulders by executing a subtle rolling movement, first pulling up your shoulders before letting them sink down. Keep your eyes closed at first and only open them once you've gone through the positions several times. Never let your head fall backward or forward in an uncontrolled manner—you always need to use some muscle strength to position your head where you want it to be.

You can do this exercise sitting or standing. It is the perfect way to relax areas that are persistently tense. Note: It is extremely important to proceed slowly and take deep breaths.

Shoulders

Lie on your side with the following parts of your body aligned at right angles: lower legs-thighs; thighs-torso; torso-chin. One arm should support your head and the other rests on your upper body with your wrist on your hip (fig. 69).

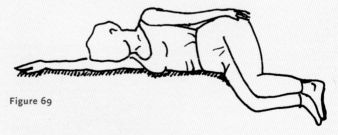

Figure 69

Move your upper shoulder as far forward as possible without forcing it. Move slowly and gently. Return to starting position. Move your shoulder backward in the same way. Finally, connect both movements in one fluid motion. Start with large, slow motions before letting them become smaller and faster until your shoulder is literally wobbling like gelatin, an inch or so in both directions (fig. 70). Repeat 10 times.

Next, pull your shoulder up to your ear before dropping it down toward your hip. Connect both movements by starting with large, slow motions before decreasing and accelerating them (fig. 71). Finish off with circular motions in both directions.

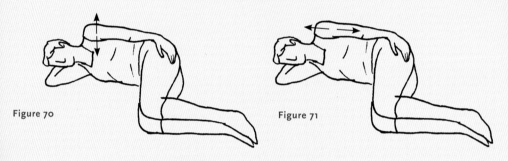

Figure 70

Figure 71

Hips

Begin in the same position as you did in the shoulder joints exercise, and proceed to follow the same steps, performing the same motions, only this time with your hips.

Knees

Sit on a chair so your thighs and knees are nearly perpendicular. You should be comfortable. Place your fingers underneath the point where your thighs and knees merge. You will feel two tendons—to the left and right of your knee. "Pinch" or "pluck" at the tendons as you have with your muscles in previous exercises (fig. 72 and photo 94).

Figure 72

94

Ankles

You can increase the flexibility of your ankles by "stimulating" your Achilles tendons. This makes the area more "spring-like" and therefore easier to flex your heels downward. In order to massage your Achilles tendon, sit on a chair and rest one foot on the knee of the opposite leg. "Pinch" and "pluck" at your Achilles tendon with your thumb and index finger (fig. 73 and photo 95).

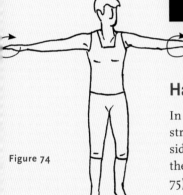

Figure 73

Hands

In a standing position with your legs slightly apart and bent, straighten your upper body and spread your arms out to either side. Move your hands in small circles (fig. 74). Then, flap them (from the wrists, not the shoulders) up and down (fig. 75). Finally, open and close your hands (fig. 76).

Figure 74

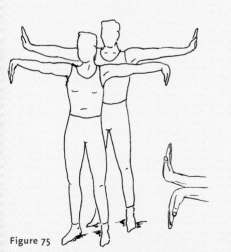

Figure 75

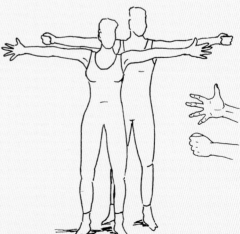

Figure 76

Integration of Joints and Other Areas of the Body

Head and Neck Area to Shoulders

Lie on your back and lift one shoulder toward the ear on the same side. Move your head toward the shoulder you are lifting (fig. 77).

Figure 77

Shoulders to Hips

Lie on your back. Push one shoulder toward the hip joint on the same side while at the same time lifting the hip toward the shoulder. Practice on both sides of your body (fig. 78).

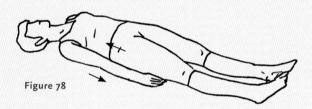

Figure 78

Dynamic Buttocks

Sitting is never static (without change) but always dynamic (continuous change). You can interrupt stereotypical sitting patterns by sitting in a chair and sliding one buttock off one side of the seat, then lifting and lowering that side of your body (fig. 79). Repeat 10 times on each side. You will experience a pleasant change in your entire body structure.

Activate New Motion Patterns for Your Head

Again sit in a chair and slide your right buttock off the seat so it is suspended in the air. Place your left foot in front of the chair while your right foot supports your center of gravity.

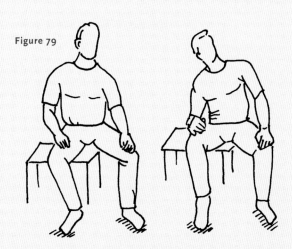

Figure 79

96

Place your right hand on your head. It is responsible for moving your head; your head should follow your hand's directions in a relaxed manner.

Move your head sideways from left to right as far as possible without straining. Do not work against your body's resistance. As you move your head, lower your right buttock below the seat, then lift it up toward your shoulder (fig. 80). Switch sides: Sit on your right buttock with the left one suspended. Position your right foot in front of the chair while the left one supports your center of gravity. Place your left hand on your head and move your head sideways from left to right as you lower and lift your buttock (photo 96). This exercise mobilizes both sides of your spine while integrating your shoulders and hips.

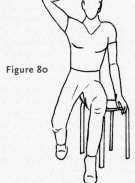

Figure 80

"Monkey Pose"—Integration of All Joints

"Monkey pose" corresponds to the forward seat on horseback. Movement is transferred from your feet all the way to your head, which mobilizes or stabilizes your entire body as needed.

Stand with your knees bent just enough that they are in front of your toes. This enables your back to stretch (fig. 81). Move your hips backward as if they are hinged, but keep your knees as they are, slightly in front of your toes (fig. 82). Hold your position. You can check your position by making sure that your lower legs and torso are parallel to each other. This parallelism is lacking in most riders when they are in a forward seat.

Assume the "monkey pose" in the saddle at the trot and canter. When trotting, your buttocks should remain suspended out of the saddle (that is, do not "sit" every other stride as when posting). At the canter, ride in forward seat with significantly shorter stirrups. These two exercises will mobilize your knee and hip joints). After performing this exercise, tense riders are considerably more relaxed; atonic, limp riders show significantly better body control ("positive" body tension).

See more exercises in the saddle in Part Two, beginning on p. 172.

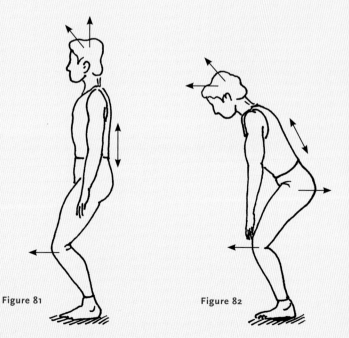

Figure 81   Figure 82

Workout 7: Axial Rotation and Cross-Coordination

This workout specifically prepares you for what I call the "rotational seat"—turning your body as you ride your horse on curved lines (such as circles and turns). It is a particularly important workout for riders who tend to ride with an "open body"—that is, in turns, their outside (outside the bend) shoulder lags behind, and their shoulders and pelvis are no longer parallel to the horse's. When you ride with an "open body," you are unable to follow the horse's movements in an optimal fashion.

The exercises presented in Workout 7 will subconsciously teach you cross-coordination and how to use it at all times without even thinking about it. The better your axial rotation and the more automatic your cross-coordination, the better able you are to follow your horse's movements and the more targeted your reactions can be in certain situations.

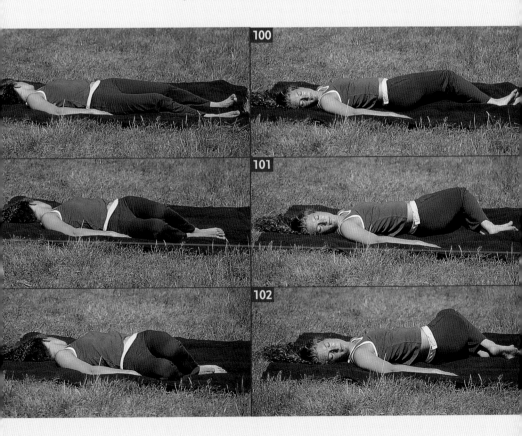

The following exercises not only address your body but also prepare your brain in the best way possible so nerve impulses can get to your muscles more quickly and accurately.

Working Your Body

Lie on your back with your legs stretched out before you. Bend your knees slightly so your heels move about 4 inches closer to your buttocks. Slowly move your knees sideways from left to right until they touch the floor. Turn your head in the direction opposite that toward which you are moving your knees. Repeat 10 times before moving your feet another 4 inches closer to your buttocks, and doing the exercise again. Continue moving your heels closer and repeating the movements until the soles of your feet are flat on the ground (photos 97–102). At this point, begin to gradually move your heels away from your buttocks until your legs are lying straight on the floor again.

Opposite Movements

The following exercises should be practiced in both directions and repeated at least 8 to 10 times.

EXERCISE 1 (EYES VS. HEAD):
Begin in the same position as you did in the last exercise. Turn your head to the right while turning your eyes to the left, and vice versa (fig. 83).

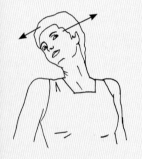

Figure 83

EXERCISE 2 (ARMS VS. HEAD):
Begin in the same position as in Exercise 1. Fold your hands and stretch out your arms so they are perpendicular to your body. Turn your head right while moving your outstretched arms in the opposite direction until they touch the floor (fig. 84). Repeat in opposite direction.

EXERCISE 3 (SHOULDERS VS. HEAD):
Begin in the same position as in Exercise 1. Cross your arms in front of your chest, with your hands on your shoulders. With the help of your hands, turn your shoulders to the left while turning your head to the right, and vice versa (fig. 85). Do not actively move your shoulders—use your hands to move them, instead.

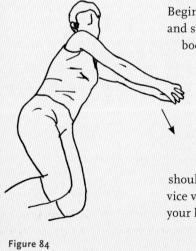

Figure 84

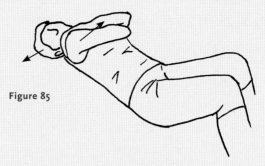

Figure 85

EXERCISE 4 (HEAD VS. SHOULDERS):

Lie flat on your stomach, stretch out your legs, and cross your arms in front of you so your forehead can rest on them. Turn your head to the left while moving your right shoulder (and elbow) to the right, and vice versa (fig. 86).

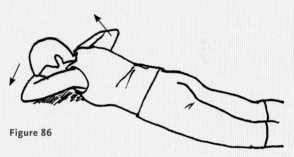

Figure 86

EXERCISE 5 (HEAD VS. HIPS):

Lie flat on your back and bend your knees so your feet are flat on the floor. While lifting your right hip over toward the left, turn your head to the right, and vice versa (figs. 87 A & B).

Figure 87 A

Figure 87 B

EXERCISE 6 (ARMS VS. HIPS):

Begin as you did in Exercise 5. Fold your hands and stretch your arms upward until they are perpendicular to your body. While moving your arms to the left toward the floor, lift your left hip toward the right side of your body, and vice versa (fig. 88).

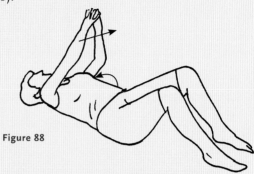

Figure 88

EXERCISE 7 (SHOULDERS VS. HIPS):

Begin as you did in Exercise 5. Cross your arms in front of your chest and place your hands on your shoulders. Do not actively move your shoulders but use your hands instead. With the help of your hands, turn your shoulders to the left while turning your left hip to the right, and vice versa (fig. 89).

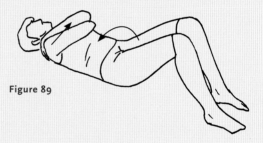

Figure 89

EXERCISE 8 (HEAD VS. HIPS):

Lie flat on your stomach, bend your knees at a right angle so your lower legs are perpendicular to your body, and cross your arms in front of your head so you can rest your forehead on your hands. While turning your head to the right, lift your right hip, and vice versa (fig. 90).

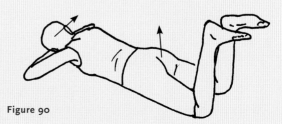

Figure 90

EXERCISE 9 (SHOULDERS VS. HIPS):

Begin on your stomach as in Exercise 8. Simultaneously, lift your right hip and left shoulder (and elbow) off the ground, and vice versa (fig. 91).

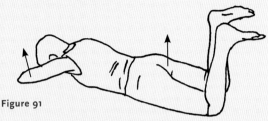

Figure 91

EXERCISE 10 (HEAD VS. KNEES):

Lie on your back, bend your knees and pull your feet close to your body. Your legs should be slightly apart. Turn your legs to one side while keeping them parallel to each other. At the same time, turn your head in the opposite direction (fig. 92). Practice on both sides of your body.

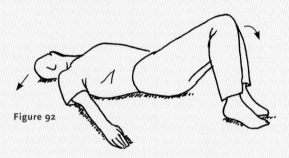

Figure 92

EXERCISE 11 (ARMS VS. KNEES):

Begin on your back with your knees bent, as in Exercise 10, this time with your hands joined and your arms stretched out over your head. Turn your legs to one side while keeping them parallel to each other. At the same time, move your outstretched arms in the opposite direction toward the floor (fig. 93). Practice on both sides of your body.

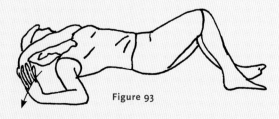

Figure 93

EXERCISE 12 (SHOULDERS VS. KNEES):

Begin as in Exercise 10 but this time cross your arms over your chest. Turn your legs to one side while keeping them parallel to each other. At the same time, use your hands to pull your shoulders in the opposite direction (fig. 94). Practice on both sides of your body.

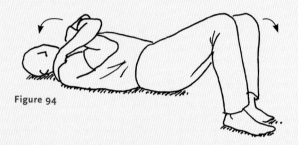

Figure 94

EXERCISE 13 (LEGS VS. HEAD):

Lie flat on your stomach, bend your knees so your lower legs are perpendicular to your body, cross your arms underneath your head, and rest your forehead on your hands. Your legs should be slightly apart with the soles of your feet facing the ceiling. Keep your lower legs parallel as you move to one side toward the floor (figs. 95 A & B). Repeat the exercise, this time turning your nose in the same direction as you are moving your lower legs (fig. 96). Again repeat the movement, now turning your head in the opposite direction of your legs (fig. 97). Practice on both sides of your body.

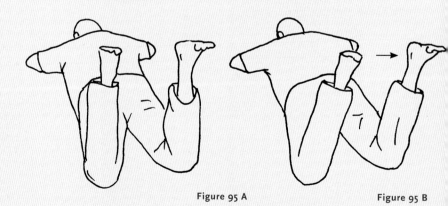

Figure 95 A   Figure 95 B

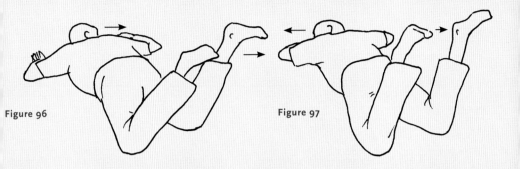

Figure 96   Figure 97

EXERCISE 14:

Raise the level of difficulty of Exercises 10 through 12 by resting one foot on the opposite knee instead of moving your legs parallel to each other (fig. 98).

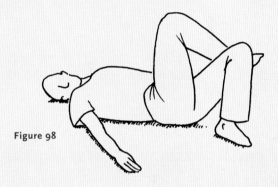

Figure 98

EXERCISE 15:

Lie on your side with a pillow supporting your head. Position your body so your torso and thighs, and thighs and lower legs are at a right angle. Move your top leg slightly further forward than the bottom leg so both knees can touch the floor (make sure they maintain this contact through all the exercises). Stretch your arms out in front of you so they are perpendicular to your torso, and place one palm in the other.

Lift your upper arm until it is stretched vertically above you, then lower it back to the floor. At first, your head should not change position (fig. 99). After several repetitions, move your head so your eyes follow the movement of your hand (fig. 100). Repeat, alternating the two movements, then move your arm as far back as possible (keeping it at shoulder level) without straining. All movements should be smooth and easy.

Figure 99

Figure 100

Again repeat with your head following the motion, and then alternating both movements (fig. 101). You will notice that it becomes easier and easier to move your arm backward until it finally touches the floor behind you (fig. 102). Practice with both arms.

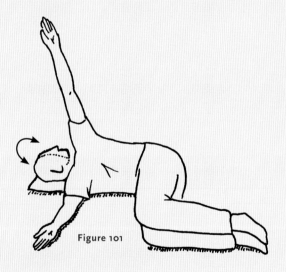

Figure 101

EXERCISE 16:

Begin on your side positioned as in Exercise 15. Move your upper arm in a circular motion: over your head, behind your back, over your hip and back to its starting position (fig. 103). The hand of the opposite arm and your knees should maintain

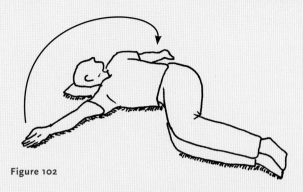

Figure 102

contact with the floor, which might be very difficult in the beginning. The more often you practice, the better contact you will be able to maintain with the floor. At first, your head should not move, but after several repetitions, allow your eyes to follow the movements of your upper arm and hand.

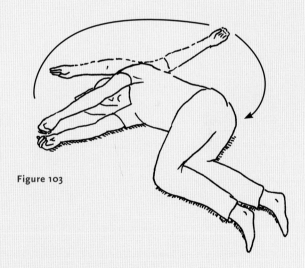

Figure 103

The Cool-Down Process

Active "De-Tiring"

During your cool-down after you ride, you can use the same exercises you used to warm up off the horse. They target all major muscle groups, which helps eliminate (negative) tension and rid your body of metabolic waste. In addition, you can choose a few exercises from the workouts on pp. 33–93 to address specific problem areas.

You should make use of various relaxation techniques in order to process positive and negative events that may have occurred during your riding session. This is especially helpful with regard to competition, as such a "mental cool-down" helps you free yourself from reliving the competition experience. Most riders are familiar with nights of fitful sleep directly following competition, in which they relive their performance over and over again. Therefore, autogenic training or progressive muscle relaxation should be included in your cool-down phase.

Autogenic Training

Autogenic training, according to German psychiatrist Johannes Heinrich Schultz, consists of a series of exercises that help your body transition into a state of passive concentration. A typical training session starts with you assuming a comfortable sitting posture (either reclined or upright with your head lowered) or lying flat on your back with your knees bent. Close your eyes.

Begin with a breathing warm-up while you mentally tell yourself, "I am completely calm," in order to relax your mind and body. Continue with the following exercises (or phases), during which you have to seriously try and become aware of and feel different body parts:

1 HEAVINESS:
Your right (left) arm feels really heavy. Use this statement to label individual parts as you work through your entire body. **Goal:** Muscle relaxation, general calmness.

2 WARMTH:
Your right (left) arm feels really warm. Now use this statement to label individual body parts one after the other. **Goal:** Relaxation of blood vessels, general relaxation.

3 CALM HEART:
Your heartbeat is calm and absolutely steady.
Goal: Normalization of heart activity, relaxation.

4 BREATHING:
You breathe slowly and steadily. **Goal:** Your breathing
becomes harmonious and passive, you become relaxed.

5 STOMACH:
Your stomach feels radiantly warm. **Goal:** Harmonization
of all abdominal viscera, relaxation.

6 COOL FOREHEAD:
Your forehead feels pleasantly cool. **Goal:** Cool and clear head,
relaxation of all blood vessels in the head, general relaxation.

Progressive Muscle Relaxation

Progressive muscle relaxation (PMR) involves the tensing and
relaxing of muscle groups in a predetermined order. Here I
provide the basics of this technique, which you can use after
a riding lesson or competition as part of your cool-down.

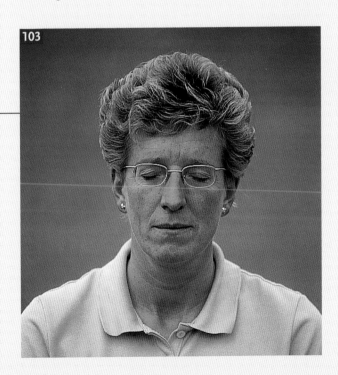

Photo 103 *Telling yourself,
"I am completely calm,"
following your riding session,
is the first step when incorporating autogenic training
in your cool-down.*

Tense up every muscle group only as long as you need to realize the tension you have created. This takes about 5 to 8 seconds. Until you have developed a feeling for this period of time, count the seconds as they pass. You need to create tension, become aware of it, and then relax the tensed area. As you do so, concentrate on improving your awareness of and feel for the respective muscles.

Proceed in the following order:
1 Dominant hand and forearm
2 Dominant upper arm
3 Nondominant hand and forearm
4 Nondominant upper arm
5 Forehead
6 Upper cheeks and nose
7 Lower cheeks and chin
8 Nape area and neck
9 Chest, shoulders, and upper back
10 Abdominal muscles
11 Dominant thigh
12 Dominant lower leg
13 Dominant foot
14 Nondominant thigh
15 Nondominant lower leg
16 Nondominant foot

Part 2

Exercise Routines on Horseback
*Improving Suppleness, Flexibility, and Coordination
in the Saddle*

The Basics of the Training Scale

The Training Scale—The Horse

The Classical Training Scale is considered by many to be the primary schooling guide for any serious horse trainer and rider. In order to train horses for under-saddle work in a healthy and natural way, the Training Scale offers a series of principles that consist of irreversible interdependencies. If you do not follow the Training Scale's structure, you will likely suffer the consequences at some point during your horse's schooling. Sooner or later, mistakes and shortfalls will inhibit further progress altogether, or it will only be achieved at the expense of your horse and his health.

A horse living and moving around in the wild according to his instincts and via his natural mode of locomotion does not need the Training Scale. As soon as you start riding your horse, you are interfering with his instincts and natural movements. This means that you have to reestablish them on a secondary level; riding theory helps you in your efforts by providing you with the Training Scale.

Training and riding horses is in no way cruel to the animals as many "non-horsey" people might think. As a matter of fact, classical riding is the best form of physical training a horse will ever receive—its premise is to build up his body in a healthy way and enable him to perform his best. Let's take a look at the principles that make up this method of schooling the horse.

Rhythm and Suppleness = "Familiarization Phase"

In order to show regular rhythm in all gaits under saddle, horses need to get used to carrying a rider on their back. This can be a problem when a horse stands in a stall all day. Horses are herd animals and move constantly if given the chance to; when "contained" in a stall, they stand too much and become tense, which leads to irregularities in rhythm during the first couple of minutes of riding.

This is where you as a rider come in—you need to influence your horse and restore his rhythm with your own regular movements. (Possible only if you warmed up sufficiently prior to riding.) To go further, horses can become relaxed and supple in mind and body only if their movements are absolutely regular. Therefore, rhythm and suppleness are the

Photo 104 *This horse is demonstrating a nice stretching posture.*

basis of all further training; they are the goal of the first phase of the Training Scale, which is often called the "familiarization phase."

Contact and Impulsion = Developing Pushing Power

Once rhythm and suppleness have been established, the horse's movement will start to show a forward tendency—in other words, "pushing power." Pushing power describes the process during which the horse develops energy in his hindquarters (impulsion) and sends it forward toward the contact established between his mouth and the rider's hands. This impulsion and contact make up the second phase in a horse's training.

The rider needs to be very sensitive and finely regulate this energy. She needs to establish a balance of energy between her forward-driving and regulating aids. No one aid should dominate all the others—although unfortunately, this can often be observed in riders who apply constant non-yielding rein aids or push their horse forward relentlessly (usually at too high a speed with little or no contact). These riders fail to fine-tune their aid applications and concentrate too much on their hands.

Straightness and Collection = Developing Carrying Power

The goal of the third phase in the Training Scale is to correct a horse's natural crookedness—and achieve straightness—as well as to develop collection (wherein the horse shifts more of his weight to his hindquarters). Every horse is born "crooked," which is not an issue as long as he lives his life without facing the demands of being a riding horse. Once a rider puts weight on the horse's back, however, things change.

Photo 105 *Olympian Heike Kemmer demonstrates a lateral weight aid.*

The energy produced in the hindquarters (pushing power) cannot directly flow forward through the horse's body if his forehand is not aligned with his hindquarters. All energy needs to travel from the croup, through the spine, and to the horse's mouth. When that is not the case, the potential energy produced in the hindquarters simply vanishes into thin air. In addition, as is the case with human athletes, when a riding horse is inherently crooked and the issue is not addressed, his spine gets distorted and he often ends up injured. Moreover, horses cannot learn to "carry themselves" when their bodies are not straight.

The bottom line? The Training Scale is based on the assumption that well-trained riders will consistently ride their inexperienced horses according to a proven structure so that their equine partners can learn and develop in a way that is healthy and natural. Whenever horse and rider come together in a teaching-and-learning environment, one or the other needs to be able to show his or her partner the path to educational success. In this case, the rider is the teacher while the horse is the student.

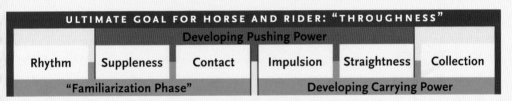

Source: *Die Skala der Ausbildung* (the scales of training) by Britta Schöffmann

The Training Scale—The Rider

The training of riders can be organized as a scale in the same way as the training of horses. The most important requirement with regard to the rider's development is that the methodical path of the rider's training is designed in a way that enables her to recognize gaps in her education caused by unfamiliar situations. The rider must be confident that she will be able to "fill in" these gaps working with her horse or horses and with the support of her instructor. Ideally her horse has already successfully completed the respective step of the equine Training Scale (see p. 102). The horse needs to have been correctly trained according to classical riding theory so his motion sequences allow his rider to feel what specific movements

▶ To be of benefit, the "Rider Training Scale" must be consistently followed.

are supposed to feel like. This is the only way in which riders will be able to develop a "feel" for movements, complex aid application, and subtle influence while on horseback.

When learning a new sport, people always fall back on motion patterns they are already familiar with and transfer them to the unfamiliar learning situation (cf. Chatzopoulos 1997, Egger 1975, Kassat 1998, Leist 1975, 2002). Motion patterns are defined as approaches to structurally similar movements, techniques, or motions required in specific situations. For example, when a person wants to learn a technique in badminton (serving from the rear court), she will resort to motion sequences she might already have learned playing tennis (serve). In fact, the only thing she has to learn from scratch is the difference in how you use your wrist—very high wrist action in badminton; almost none in tennis. Other necessary movements will "run" as internalized (automated).

▸ The sport of riding is unique in its motion patterns and posture— it is not easily compared to actions of any other athletic endeavor.

Rider Training Scale

ULTIMATE GOAL FOR HORSE AND RIDER: "THROUGHNESS"

Rider Abilities ◂—▸ Rider Skill

The rider needs to mentally, emotionally, and physically prepare herself for riding.	The rider has to develop balance, rhythm in her movements, and "feel" for the horse's motion. She must be able to apply aids at a basic skill level in order to support the horse's pushing power.	Riders must be able to ride "actively"—that is, use aids in all their complexity in order to achieve control over their horse.
The horse needs to be able to adjust to the rider's weight in order to find rhythm and suppleness.	The horse must not be unbalanced or blocked in his effort to develop pushing power.	The horse should be straightened and collected with the help of the aids so he can develop carrying power.
Phase One: Familiarization	**Phase Two: Developing Pushing Power**	**Phase Three: Developing Carrying Power**

We transfer elements we already know and abilities we already have to situations or techniques we are not yet familiar with. In this way, we make learning a little easier on ourselves since we only have to focus on the new aspects. This acceleration of new learning due to prior experience is called positive transfer. However, it is also important to know that motion patterns we have already internalized that have no structural connection to the new technique or situation can interfere

> General skills and abilities such as balance, rhythm, and a "feel" for motion are integral to the sport of riding. They are the basis for developing specific riding techniques. Skills and abilities are generally non-specific to sporting discipline, while techniques can usually only be applied to one sport.

with our ability to learn and improve, otherwise known as negative transfer.

With regard to learning how to ride, transfer is not applicable as there aren't any sports, situations, or skills that are structurally similar to riding. In our society, the posture and position used when riding is unique and is not easily compared to any other athletic motion or sport system. Instead, the structural basis of riding relies on the abilities necessary when in destabilizing situations (where we lose body stability) and related problem-solving skills. In this way, riding is similar to skiing and surfing (although participants in those sports do experience positive and negative transfer).

Due to all I've described thus far, the steps of the Rider Training Scale do not include specific motion patterns, but instead try to help you master the basic abilities you must have in order to achieve and maintain internal and external stability in all situations—both everyday life and athletic endeavor.

The structure of the Rider Training Scale presented in this book is based, among others, on the findings of Dr. Anna Jean Ayres and her work in occupational therapy and brain research (cf. Ayres 1998, Chatzopoulos 1997, Hirtz/Hotz/Ludewig 2003, Kirchner/Pöhlmann 2005, Loosch 1999, Meinel/Schnabel 2007, Weineck 2007). At first, we will focus on general skills, which will be transformed into techniques (aid application and control) during the course of the rider's development. Even though each phase includes basic aid application and certain aspects of control, complex aiding will only be introduced after all basic skills (balance, rhythm, "feel" for motion) have been mastered.

Phase One—Familiarization

As we've discussed, I feel the training of riders should be determined by a system or structure in the same way the schooling of horses is—that is, via a "Training Scale." The first phase of the Rider Training Scale—the "familiarization" phase—serves as a period in which you get used to your horse, his movements and your movements in specific situations, and your instructor's style of teaching.

Your horse's behavior and personality must be such that you feel safe riding him, and your instructor needs to be your "partner" in your in-saddle endeavors, as well. Your instructor should have a positive psychological effect on you so you are

Photo 106 *Heike rotates her head and shoulders in opposite directions.*

▸ Trust in your instructor, your horse, and in yourself ultimately leads to a supple body and relaxed mind when in the saddle.

open to her ideas and support during training sessions. An instructor's educational approach and riding curriculum starts with her personality—regardless of her professional qualifications, she will only be a successful teacher if you can willingly and completely accept her leadership.

Ultimately, you should only get on your horse when you meet the following criteria:
▸ You have absolutely no fear of your horse.
▸ You are not frightened of your instructor, and you respect her methods and approach.
▸ You can leave your everyday problems at home, or "on the ground" so you can fully and open-mindedly engage in the riding process.

Photo 107 *It is important to feel comfortable with your instructor in order to get the most from your lessons.*

Any negative emotion, thought, or tension will interfere in such a significant way that you will not be able to relax and let your horse move (and thus move you) or correctly apply aids. And, if you lack suppleness of body and tranquility of mind, it is impossible for your horse to move rhythmically or relax.

> ▶ You must leave negative thoughts and experiences behind when you get in the saddle. Stress and good riding are mutually exclusive.

A "negative state of mind" results in constant muscle contractions inside your body. In fact, every emotion leads to a muscle contraction; if the emotion is positive, it will cause a contraction followed by an immediate release. Positive muscular interplay is rhythmical. However, negative emotions and thoughts lead to constant subconscious contractions that interfere with your rhythm of motion. You will find yourself out of sync with your horse because you are unable to relax and really "sit" in the saddle. You will also suffer from balance problems.

> ▶ Overly intense concentration leads to negative tension, which is detrimental in the saddle.

Stressors also obstruct internal coordination processes so your cerebral hemispheres (left and right brain) fail to correspond with their respective half of the body—normally, the left cerebral hemisphere controls the right side of your body, and vice versa. A stressed or negative state of mind disrupts emotional balance to the point that you turn into what I call a "pacer"—someone who lacks left-right coordination in her movements.

Our inclination to "concentrate," sometimes too intensely, creates an inflexible inner state that leads to tunnel vision; in other words, your field of vision is compromised to the extent that you are no longer able to perceive the world around you in its entirety.

Phase Two: Developing Pushing Power

The Effect of "Emotional Imbalance" on Your Physical Balance

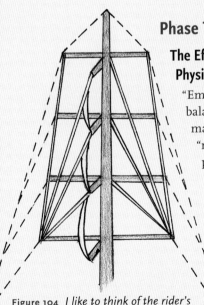

"Emotional imbalance" quickly leads to a loss of physical balance, as well. I like to think of the rider's body as a mast and sails on a ship (fig. 104). The idea behind this "mast model" is that any kind of change in one body part immediately leads to change in the entire system. For example, fear (an "emotional imbalance") usually shows as a tilting of the shoulders sideways or forward. This change in shoulder posture automatically affects the complex tension/relaxation relationships in your body and leads to positional shifts, not only in your chest area, but also in your hips, knees, and even your feet.

When using the mast model, you must take into consideration that the human "mast"— the spine—is not stable but very much the

Figure 104 *I like to think of the rider's body as a ship's mast and sails, wherein a change in one body part ultimately affects the entire system.*

▶ To ride well, you have to be emotionally, cognitively, and muscularly balanced.

opposite; it is quite flexible. Therefore, when psychological pressure drains your muscles' ability to keep you balanced, your physical (muscular) imbalances (that is, differences in strength) become even more problematic.

108

Short and tight

Weakened

Short and tight

Short and tight

Weakened

Short and tight

Short and tight

Weakened

Short and tight

Short and tight

Short and tight

Weakened

Photo 108 Heike Kemmer demonstrates typical areas of weakening and shortening/tightening of muscles in riders.

Causes, Locations, and Prevention of Muscular Imbalances

Every rider shows muscular imbalances, which lead to weaknesses and mistakes in her riding. Cultural development has caused our society to move less and in ways that differ from our ancestors. The general lack of movement in modern life; abnormal biomechanical stress; overuse and misuse; and lack of exercise further shorten (and disproportionately so) those muscles naturally prone to tightening.

When inactivity, neglect, and incorrect exercise practice weaken those muscles even more that are already prone to be-

► Regular exercise routines can get rid of muscular imbalances.

Figure 105 *1) Anterior tibialis; 2) Gastrocnemius and soleus (calf muscles).*

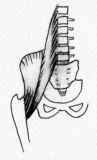

Figure 106 *Psoas major and iliacus (hip flexors).*

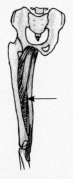

Figure 107 *Adductors (inner thigh muscles).*

ing weak, these muscles need to receive particular strength training in order to prevent imbalances from becoming even more severe. We also need to reverse the effect of our shortened muscles by stretching them.

Legs

In today's world, our calf muscles are usually shortened and tight while the *anterior tibialis* muscle tends to be weak (fig. 105). As a result, we have difficulty lowering our heels while riding. (Another common cause of this problem is a lack of mobility of the hip joints.)

The anterior (front) thigh muscles are highly prone to shortening. Since their opponents, the posterior (back) thigh muscles, are often shortened at the same time, knee problems are common as the increase in muscle tension causes pain in this joint. The inner thigh muscles (adductors) are also often affected. As a result, every rider has a potential tendency to pinch with the knees and thighs because the opposing muscles (gluteal muscles/abductors) are usually weak and incapable of countering the pinching movement (see more about these below).

Pelvis and Buttocks

The rider's "motion center"—the pelvis—is connected to many different muscles that can interfere with your ability to follow your horse's movements. The hip flexors and adductors tend to be short and tight (figs. 106 and 107). They make the pelvis tip forward, cause a hollow back, and can increase the tendency to lean forward with your upper body.

The gluteal muscles are responsible for parting the legs while the adductors press them together and pull them upward (fig. 108). In order to have as "long" a leg as possible and to rhythmically apply aids as necessary, you really have to stretch your hip flexors and strengthen your gluteal muscles (provided your hip joints are flexible).

Abdomen and Back

In today's society, human abdominal muscles are usually weak. Supported by the gluteal and posterior thigh muscles, their task is to stabilize the pelvis. And as mentioned previously, if your pelvis position is incorrect, your riding seat will never be perfectly efficient or stable. The abdominal internal

Figure 108 *Gluteal muscles.*

Figure 109 *Abdominal muscles.*

Figure 110 *Erector spinae muscles.*

and external oblique muscles are necessary for good and influential posture on horseback, as they maintain your shoulder position (fig. 109).

Your erector spinae muscles from the thoracic to the lumbar vertebrae stretch your spine and greatly influence your upright posture when in the saddle. (Again, the prerequisite for a straight spine is correct positioning of the pelvis.) In the cervical and lumbar region, the erector spinae muscles tend to become shortened and tight, which results in a hollow back or tight shoulders, while in the thoracic vertebrae, these muscles are usually weaker, which leads to a rounded back (maybe even a humpback) because our chest muscles are usually very strong and pull forward the upper part of our torso.

The superficial back muscles (the muscles of the shoulder girdle, specifically the trapezius) show two tendencies. The lower section of the muscles of the shoulder girdle shorten and thus cause the shortening of the erector spinae muscles in the lumbar region of the back; this often leads to a hollow back. The middle and upper parts of the shoulder girdle muscles tend to be weak. Since, in the thoracic area, the erector spinae tend to also be weak while the opposing pectoral muscle is usually strong, the result is a rounded back.

Many people today suffer from lateral spinal distortions, so it is all the more important to have strong lateral core muscles (specifically the psoas major) to secure an upright posture without tipping sideways. In our modern society, the lateral core muscles are generally underdeveloped, which causes many riders to collapse their hips.

Only after you have rectified existing muscular imbalances in your body will you have fulfilled the prerequisites necessary to sit balanced in the saddle—that is, perpendicular.

Balance as a Fundamental Sensory Ability

I want to emphasize the fact that balance—both mental and physical—is a human ability closely connected to all our senses. When you have problems with your balance, all your senses are negatively affected (Ayres 1998). So, when you lack balance while riding your horse, you will have a hard time using your senses' full potential to learn, practice, and train.

The need to constantly concentrate on "keeping your balance" strongly affects your eyes' ability to receive information. This makes it difficult for you to apply aids in order to execute particular exercises at specific markers in the arena, for example. Eventers and hunter/jumper riders will have a hard time finding the correct distance to a jump.

If you are struggling with your balance, you will also find it difficult to process any verbal information your riding instructor is sharing with you. When you are busy maintaining your posture, the receptivity of your hearing is significantly reduced. Moreover, all tactile and kinesthetic information is less intensely perceived.

What Does "Balance" Mean?

In the past, sport science—a discipline that studies the application of scientific principles and techniques to the betterment of sporting performance—used to differentiate between static and dynamic balance, as well as object balance. Static balance described the ability to, for example, maintain one's equilibrium when standing on one foot. If you try to stand on one foot, however, you soon realize that you have to engage in many little and large compensatory movements in order to stand as steadily as possible. Since they were constantly moving, it turned out that the term "static" (having no motion) was inappropriate.

Today, we differentiate based on the situation a person is in: standing balance, moving balance, rotary equilibrium, and balance in suspension (see p. 114). Our vestibular and kinesthetic systems are responsible for handling these situations (Bertram/Laube 2008, Hirtz/Hotz/Ludewig 2000, Hirtz/Nüske 1997, Kirchner/Pöhlmann 2005, Schöllhorn/Michelbrink/Grzybowski 2007).

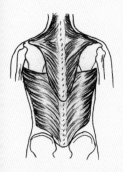

Figure 111 *The superficial back muscles.*

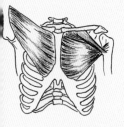

Figure 112 *The pectoral muscles.*

▶ Good balance—mental and physical—sharpens all our senses.

Photos 109 & 110
Exercises that promote cross-coordination are excellent preparation for riding, and for riding dressage specifically.

Vestibular System

The vestibular system is located in the inner ear. The vestibular system works together with other sensory organs, such as the eyes and ears, to transmit positional changes of the body to the brain so that our body can then compensate for the changes. With this system in mind, it is important that you neither move your head too far forward nor tilt it too far backward or sideways, as postures like these distort the information processed in your inner ear and compensatory movements then cannot be adjusted to the respective situations.

Kinesthetic System

The so-called "kinesthetic system" receives information from receptors located in joints, tendons, and muscles—the proprioceptors. Proprioceptors make up a self-contained, fast-reacting, functional unit that detects changes in body part position more quickly than receptors in any other sense organ (eye, ear, skin). This enables our body to instantly detect and deal with imbalances via subtle compensatory muscle movements as necessary. This happens so quickly that bystanders do not even notice your momentary loss of balance.

A prerequisite for highly sensitive vestibular and kinesthetic systems is that you move a lot and in all kinds of ways. Only if you constantly stimulate ("train") both systems can you develop them as best as possible and keep them able to perform well. Unfortunately, physical activity in humans, beginning in childhood and continuing through adolescence and into adulthood, has been in steady decline, so we more and more often lack the basic indispensable skills riding—a sport reliant on balance—requires (see more about kinesthesia on p. 117).

As an aside: For the reasons just discussed, I am of the opinion that all riding instructors should have a background in teaching physical education that enables them to correctly prepare someone for a balanced position in the saddle. They should be able to apply and impart the latest scientific methods based on body awareness, perception, and teaching/learning techniques (Bertram/Laube 2008, Hirtz/Hotz/Ludewig 2000, Kolb 1994, Schöllhorn 2003, Schöllhorn/Michelbrink/Grzybowsky 2007).

Photo 111 *Heike Kemmer demonstrates balance in suspension.*

Different Forms of Balance

Standing balance is part of a child's natural development and is

Photo 112 *Riding requires a general state of equilibrium so you can concentrate on and cooperate with your horse.*

▶ Riding requires coordination.

the basis to building a healthy personality (self-esteem and self-identity). It is representative of your physical and emotional balance, and is a skill that often begins to deteriorate as you age. It is commonly tested with a simple exercise, such as standing on one leg. Moving balance is what you use while walking. Riders, however, use theirs in a sitting position, on top of a horse. Moving balance has to be well-developed in riders. Rotary equilibrium describes the ability to spin around without having to resort to gross motor movements of the arms and hands in order to maintain balance. Finally, balance in suspension describes a person's ability to lift her-or-himself off the ground, be suspended in the air, and land safely without losing the upright posture of their body midline.

In terms of riding, staying balanced in each of these areas is of varying importance (which I will discuss in more detail later in this book), but important just the same. The goal of general equilibrium, or balance, is genuine, since a person struggling with maintaining her balance (in any area) cannot pay any attention to other challenges and is limited in her ability to learn new movements. Riding requires a high number of little movements, both in your own body and in contact with your horse. So, when you struggle with staying balanced, you ultimately face great difficulties with regard to coordinating your body and cooperating with your horse.

In terms of physical education, coordination is defined as the muscular interplay of all partial movements that make up a certain motion. In riders, this means harmony amongst their individual body segments, and also in combination with the horse's movements. Due to the fact that learning, practicing, and training a horse specific riding exercises consists of more "partial movements" than many other sports, the art of equitation is considered a "multi-tasking" activity. So, in order to maximize ability in an efficient manner, the instructor should never address two issues at once, as human beings can only process and implement one thing at a time (due to functional limitation of the left cerebral hemisphere—Dennison 2004, Volger 1990). When you combine two or more tasks for horse and rider, important motion sequences will break down without the rider understanding exactly why. The rider's efforts to perfect her motor skills must result in her body being able to function without her having to constantly think about it ("automatically"); this way she can focus her full attention on her horse and the exercises at hand (Groeben/Wolters 2005, Wolters 2006).

▶ The sport of riding con-
fronts you with many tasks
at the same time.

Balance and Rhythm

The ability to balance and move rhythmically are mutually dependent. This means that a rider can only move rhythmically if her emotions, muscle development, and vestibular and kinesthetic systems are balanced. If she lacks balance, her motions will be irregular; every irregularity is a sign of a lack of balance. Thus, it is obvious that the ability to move rhythmically has to be the next step in the Rider Training Scale—following balance.

I want to emphasize, however, that irregularities in rhythm can be caused by physical issues. This often makes it difficult for the instructor to determine whether a student's mistake in a given situation is caused by lack of balance or a physical imbalance/blockage that needs to be addressed.

Rhythm in Motion

Generally speaking, rhythm is defined as the fluctuation and/or variation marked by the regular recurrence or flow of related elements. In riding, it is about the regularity of flexion and relaxation movements in the rider's body—in general and in specific parts.

▶ Balance is the basis of a rider's rhythm.

Rhythm can be further defined as object rhythm and subject rhythm. The horse will determine object rhythm for his rider. At first, due to his composition (height, musculature, temperament), he can only move in the way he does in a certain situation. The rider must adjust to and accept the horse's object rhythm in order to interact harmoniously with him. Only if you begin by following your horse's rhythm, will you eventually be able to use your body (subject rhythm) to change his (object rhythm) so he will start moving in a way considered optimal by classical riding theory. The large mass (horse) always moves the small mass (rider). During rising trot, the coordinated relationship between horse and rider rhythm is especially clear. The external indicator of perfect rhythm is a constant, gentle, and harmonious flow of motion during transitions and repetitions of movement. Both rhythms unite—they merge (Meinel/Schnabel 2007).

Only after you have established balance and rhythm as I've discussed, will you be able to "feel"; only then will you be able to completely adjust to and follow your horse's movements. You will have created the basis necessary to sense your horse's motion, which originates in his back, and is met by your pelvis and reciprocated. In other words, you are constantly feeling and influencing your horse.

► Riders must employ a variety of abilities to maintain a regular rhythm in the saddle.

Feeling for Motion (Kinesthesia)

Sport science has only been discussing the term kinesthesia—often interchangeably with proprioception—for the last 20 years, since it had strong emotional rather than rational connotations (it has to do with "sensing" where the parts of one's body are positioned). It is a key component in muscle memory and hand-eye coordination, especially as regards motion. Today, kinesthesia is illuminated from several different perspectives, which we will briefly discuss in the following paragraphs.

► Balance and rhythm are one.

113

Photo 113 *Horse and rider in harmony.*

Kinesthesia, or "feeling for motion," is described as a process of perception and sensation. With regard to riding, the term means the perception of the relations between space, time, and tension in one's own movements in connection with the horse's. Kinesthesia is about perceiving the individual

Kinesthesia means:
- Feeling for perception.
- Awareness of motion.
- Mental composure.
- Unity of sensing and effecting.
- Ability to differentiate between emotions.

parts of motion sequences in both your own body and your horse's, or about "feeling" a movement as a whole (interplay). In the latter case, all your senses are required to work together (for example, sight, sound, touch).

The basis for using your senses to ride your horse in a subtle and sensitive manner is the ability to be aware of your own body. You need to use your body in a way that is appropriately adjusted to a given situation, while always being aware of both your potential and limitations. You have to experience states of tension and relaxation, and feel how far you can extend your body in any direction. This is called body awareness. If you are aware of your body, you will also be aware of how it feels in different situations, which enables you to sense how you can best influence your horse.

Motion qualities such as suppleness, ease, solidity, precision, and harmony are closely connected to kinesthesia. They are present in any physical action. Kinesthesia also describes a way in which to perceive emotional states—for example, the feeling of delight when your horse dramatically extends his strides or effortlessly jumps a fence. It should be noted that fear also relates to kinesthesia, so it is not only pleasant motion or experience that elicits a sensation.

Kinesthesia always needs to be understood as the unity of perception and motion, of both "feeling" and effecting. It describes a harmonious "dialogue" between you and your horse, a process of "empathetic connection and response and sensitive contact" (Leist/Loibl 1993). You are unaware of whether you perceive a situation in a certain way because you move, or whether you move because you perceive in a certain way. The connection is not causally determined, however. (In other words, reasoned: "If I move in this way, I will feel like this...")

Photo 114 *To ride with "feel" is an elusive but worthy goal.*

Riding with "Feel"

Your "feeling for motion" is determined by the quality of your own movements. For example, if you execute your movements on horseback really well, your instructor may say that you are riding with "feel." But in reality it depends upon suppleness in both you and your horse, as well as the fusion of your movements with your horse's (the unity of your rhythms—see p. 120). An educated instructor recognizes someone riding with "feel" by the fact that the movements of horse and rider look "coherent, harmonious, and practical—downright beautiful" (Trebels 1990).

Photo 115 *A happy horse after a session of sensitive riding.*

Riding with "feel" can also be described as, very simply, your ability to ride. When you have gained enough skill to make your body and your horse's do what you want without an instructor constantly telling you what to do, and when you are able to independently make decisions for yourself and your horse, and adjust to all kinds of training situations without problems, then you are riding with "feel."

Feeling for motion also includes the concept of kinesthetic awareness: Information received by receptors (proprioceptors) in muscles, tendons, and joints informs you of tension, position, and dynamics within your horse's body, as well as within your own. It allows you to coordinate motion with an awareness of body position in time and space. This information reaches the brain faster than any other sensory input, which makes it possible for you to quickly act and react in any given situation. Kinesthetic awareness is the basis for you as a rider to determine the direction, speed, and rhythm of both your body and your horse's (Meyners 2003 and 2005, Christian 1963, Ennebach 1989, Hirtz/Hotz/Ludewig 2003, Leist/Loibl 1993, Weizsäcker 1986).

Phase Three: Developing Carrying Power

Active Aid Application and Control

It is only on this last step of the Rider Training Scale that differentiated aid application moves into focus. Only when you have learned to feel what exactly is going on in your horse as a whole are you able to apply forward-driving and regulating aids in a way that is effective. Depending on your developmental stage of balance, rhythm, and kinesthesia, you should be able to actively control and influence your horse with the help of aids.

The Interwoven Training Scales of Horse and Rider

While going through the stages of the Rider Training Scale, you will (necessarily) be applying aids at every step. The complexity of your aids, however, increases during the course of the individual schooling phases, perhaps starting on the longe line and eventually progressing to independent riding. On the longe line you will face situations in which you must learn how to apply weight, leg, and rein aids at a basic level. This is about becoming aware of your actions (aids) and your horse's reactions to them. This connection between "feeling" and effecting (Meyners 1998, 2003, 2005) is the basis for developing an understanding of how your horse moves, how his motion is passed on to your own body, and which of your physical actions are enhanced or restricted by your horse's motion.

▶ The Rider Training Scale needs to be seen as interwoven with the Classical Training Scale for the horse.

During this phase, the main task of the instructor is to present the student with exercises in which the student learns to feel the extent to which the movements of horse and rider are interwoven, as well as gains an understanding of the reasons for this phenomenon. While working on the longe line, as well as in simple situations where she is riding on her own, the rider needs to constantly practice aid application and control in order to fully understand (emotionally and intellectually) classical riding theory as a system. The rider needs to accept the fact that she must follow her horse's movements before she can influence and control them.

The instructor must always be a consultant and moderator instead of someone simply telling her students exactly what to do (Nitsch et al. 1997, Nitsch 1997). The instructor assigns a task (not a command), which the student then must try to accomplish, along with her horse. In the process, instructor and rider should discuss what the rider is feeling and experiencing. Perceptions and sensations need to be intellectually understood and transformed into reference points for future independent training. This prepares riders to make informed decisions for themselves and their horses when there is no instructor around to watch them.

Choosing Exercises According to the Rider Training Scale

116

Phase One of the Rider Training Scale can be divided into different stages that do not necessarily have to follow each other in the order I propose here. Depending on your training level or any problem areas you may have, you and/or your instructor should choose the exercises that fit your needs best. You are the most appropriate judge as to which exercises are likely most effective for your body and mind. And, your instructor should be able to tell from changes in your movements and behavior what future choices to make.

This same principle applies to Phase Two and Phase Three of the Rider Training Scale. In Phase Two, you should choose balance exercises with different focuses (muscular, kinesthetic, vestibular), depending on your problem areas, from the selection of exercises I offer on the longe line and from my 6-Point Program on horseback (see pp. 145 and 154). Your training level determines the longe line exercises that are best suited for you. Note: Longing exercises are very helpful in establishing and improving rhythm. Practicing different postures on the longe line, such as monkey pose (p. 84), and contrasting experiences, such as seat and perception exercises, helps you develop not only balance but also rhythm.

Improve muscular balance by practicing the exercises described in my 6-Point Program on horseback (see p. 154). Choose exercises that correspond to specific issues you may have. If, for example, your upper body tends to tip forward in front of the vertical, shortened pectoral muscles are most likely pulling you into this position. The muscles in your shoulder girdle are unable to compensate because they are too weak in comparison. As a result, you need to weaken your pectoral muscles (that is, trigger muscle and tendon reflexes) while, at the same time, strengthen the muscles in your shoulders. Only symmetrically and evenly developed muscles in your upper body will allow you to sit upright.

Photo 116 *This shoulder exercise is from my 6-Point Program on the ground (see p. 15).*

▶ All exercises must be adjusted to the rider's (and horse's) level of training.

▶ When you consistently experience problems with certain movements on horseback, you need a specific training routine to address the issue(s).

Since muscular imbalances reduce your ability to maintain rhythm, mobilizing the muscles in your body that tend to shorten and tighten improves both muscular balance and rhythm. This also enables you to find a common balance with your horse. Remember, you need to allow your horse's rhythm to become your own before you can use yours to influence your horse—and eventually compensate for your horse's weaknesses.

The way you apply your aids is determined by your level of sensitivity. Even though you are supposed to let your horse move you in the beginning of your rider training (the large mass always moves the small), it is your instructor's responsibility to provide you with explanations on aid application and influence—customized to your level of skills. These explanations can begin when you are still practicing on the longe line or starting your first simple schooling figures. The thorough connection of forward-driving and regulating aids, well woven together, has to be established slowly. It is the responsibility of the riding instructor to make the correct decisions regarding the complexity of exercises as is appropriate for the degree of control the rider already has.

The degree of balance, rhythm, and "feeling for motion" you have developed determines the extent to which you will be able to control (influence) your horse with the help of your aids. The aids of choice are the result of your training level.

Establishing Flexible and Stable Motion Sequences

The exercises in this book need to be executed in a specific way if you want to heighten your body awareness to such a degree that you are able to make your movements targeted and differentiated. Ideally, you will learn to be flexible in your actions/reactions and base them on a given situation. This is a fundamental skill if you want to adapt quickly to what is happening while you are in the saddle (even if it is something unexpected) and apply appropriate aids in order to control your horse in a particular moment.

▶ Using creative exercises during regular riding sessions can help certain motions come naturally to you again.

As I have mentioned throughout this book, the ideal fitness program does more than just train your body—first and foremost, it refines your brain function. Improved "self-organization" of the brain leads to better quality and variability of the

117

Photo 117 *Heike Kemmer demonstrates one of the phases of the simultaneous signs exercise (see p. 138).*

impulses that are sent to various body parts, and ultimately, improves the quality of your movements. In this context, I use the term "internalization" (incorporating subconscious or conscious guides within the self through learning) rather than "automation" (enabling a process or system to operate automatically). Internalization is about conscious perception of processes (by way of receptors, or cells that receive stimuli) and the related specific planning of actions that follow, which are then passed on to the horse. In contrast, if your motion patterns as a rider have become automated, then you are no longer able to adapt to the ever-changing conditions of riding a horse.

During your life as a rider, you will never encounter the exact same situation twice. For this reason, repeating exercises without variations is wrong—all it does is establish a stereotype of a motion pattern in your brain. This stereotype then serves as the motion pattern or "solution" in all situations, rather than just one in particular. Even though multiple repetitions of one and the same exercise, without variation, might seem to produce physical changes at first, ultimately, they only build "motion barriers" in different energetic areas such as speed and strength, or motor skills—coordination and mobility, for example (Beckmann/Schöllhorn 2006, Kolb 1994, Schöllhorn 2003, Schöllhorn et al. 2004, Schöllhorn 2005, Schöllhorn 2006, Schöllhorn et el. 2007 a, b, Schöllhorn et al. 2008).

As I explained at the beginning of this book, the goal of my fitness program is not to isolate individual muscles but to always address them in combination with other muscles that are also involved in the task as a whole (the synergy effect—the effect of multiple together is greater than the effect of one by itself). Of course, muscles can only be strengthened and stretched if trained in a nearly isolated manner. This is acceptable as long as the muscles are then reintegrated into coordinative situations (muscle chains) since the movements required of riding should be regarded holistically.

Review of the Rider Workout Principles

Keep the following guidelines in mind when doing the exercises presented in the pages that follow. You must be aware of them when learning, practicing, and training on your horse.

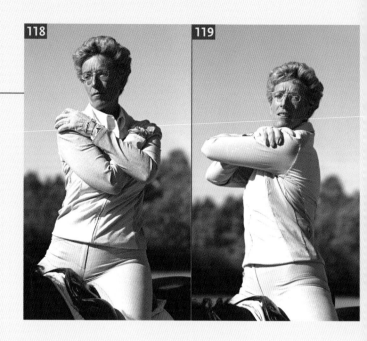

Photos 118 & 119 *Heike demonstrates rotating her head a different way than her upper body on horseback. Note how she has varied her arm position.*

Photo 120 *You can mobilize your neck area by using your hands to gently direct the head in one direction or another while you are in the saddle.*

▸ Vary tempo
▸ Vary posture
▸ Let yourself be "moved"
▸ Switch sides
▸ Vary muscular tension
▸ Focus on balance
▸ Heighten specific senses

Dealing with Your "Favorite" Side

I must emphasize the importance of performing all exercises on both sides of your body. All movements should be done with both your left and your right side in order to create muscular balance. This physical balance allows you to become more sensitive to your body and its movements, and also to coordinate motion more cohesively. Both cerebral hemispheres of the brain work in better harmony.

Every person has her "favorite side." But by favoring one side, the difference between the "strong" and "weak" side will only become increasingly pronounced. For example, if you are aware of an imbalance, do not only work on your weak side (as you might think you should) as this will not, in fact, bring about significant improvement. Your stronger side will remain implanted in your brain as such, and working more with the

Photo 121 *By varying your posture in the saddle, you can improve your balance significantly.*

Photo 122 *Closing your eyes helps you direct your focus inward.*

weaker side only reinforces the incorrect brain impulses rather than changing or improving them.

Based on what we know about transfer processes in the brain (impulses triggered in your left cerebral hemisphere influence those of the right if sides are frequently switched), you can improve your weaker side by practicing with your stronger side several consecutive times before giving your weaker side a try. After some switching, the difference will quickly become less pronounced (and often disappear completely).

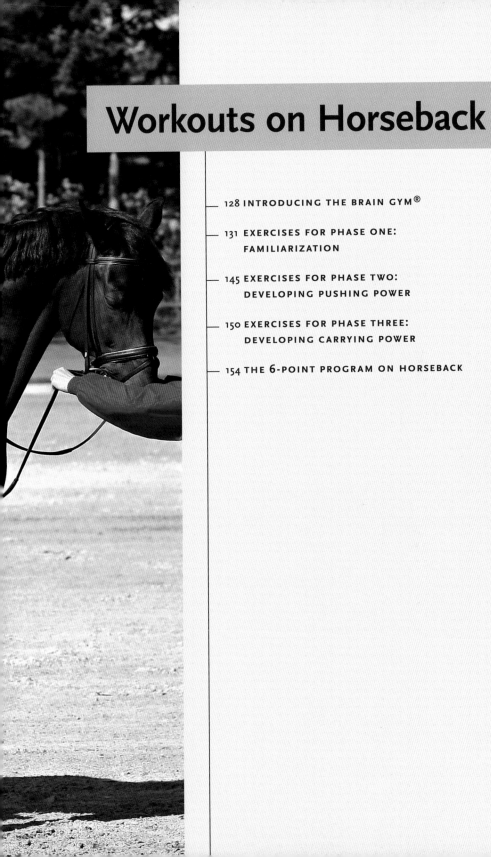

Workouts on Horseback

Introducing the Brain Gym®

The concept of the Brain Gym (educational kinesiology) was developed by educator and reading specialist Paul Dennison and his wife and colleague, Gail Dennison, in order to make learning in general much easier and to solve problems rooted in a person's subconscious (Dennison 2004, Dennison/Dennison 2006 a, b, c, Goddard 2000, Hannford 2008, Teplitz 2004). I encourage every riding instructor and rider to explore this topic beyond the fundamental aspects I provide in this book (Andrews 1998, Klingenhöffer 2005, Sterr 2006). You can learn more at www.braingym.org.

The Brain Gym relies on a set of movements or activities that recall the movements discovered in the first years of human life. Its focus is the interdependence of movement, cognition, and applied learning to improve concentration, memory, physical coordination, attitude, and more. I find that Brain Gym exercises are of great help to people (riders included) who feel stressed out. The exercises help relieve the pressure emotional problems can place on your subconscious while at the same time supporting you intensely in the process of learning something new.

▸ Every physical movement is initiated in the brain.

In the many years I have worked in this field, I have noted a few things. Since people do not move or exercise nearly enough, their sensitivity to motion patterns and motion quality has significantly decreased. Therefore, riders are often not aware of how they actually ride. They often have a distorted image of themselves; from their subjective point of view, they cannot see and perceive themselves in the same way an instructor can from the outside.

Today's rider often has a poorly developed "feeling for motion" (kinesthesia—see p. 117). You can only say that your kinesthetic sense is well developed when the "external image" (that which your instructor sees) concurs with the "internal image" you have of yourself. The more you move based on "feel" (perception-oriented), the better able you are to see yourself from the inside, recognize your skills, and detect weaknesses.

▸ The brain needs to be retrained in order to effectively lead the body.

Riders with lesser or little experience often rate themselves better than they actually are. They lack emotional self-assessment; they only use their "heads" when they ride. This means that they "overthink" while in the saddle because they are always aware of the criteria they think they need to fulfill at that point in time. In part, they might also lack motor skills and the respective motion experience (transfer—see p. 106) to fall back on when they do not know what a movement is supposed to feel like. This encourages their mind to take over and do most of the "work." Moreover, certain internal processes and actions, which would normally turn learning into a fun activity, are often missing or are subconsciously blocked by these riders.

Techniques based on the Brain Gym, and exercises related to Applied Kinesiology (see below), that I have included in this book are intended to help those who may be struggling with some of these problems.

123

Photo 123 *Lazy Eights in the saddle improve cross-coordination (see p.137).*

▶ Applied kinesiology mobilizes all of the rider's resources and makes learning easier.

What Is Applied Kinesiology?

The term kinesiology is derived from the Greek kinesis, meaning motion. Applied kinesiology (AK) is a holistic approach to the scientific study of the principles of mechanics and anatomy in relation to human movement. It is a system that evaluates structural, chemical, and mental aspects of health using a method of manual muscle testing. Both human motion and the interactions between energetic systems within our body (such as psychological and electromagnetic) are considered in an effort to reestablish an individual's equilibrium.

Photo 124 *Heike demonstrates the Thinking Cap exercise (see p. 143).*

(see p. 143)

I encourage riding instructors and riders to learn more about this method in order to make teaching easier for instructors and to support "feel"-based riding in riders. Exercises related to this concept create (near) perfect learning conditions for riders. When all your internal energetic systems are balanced, learning how to ride will be fun and you will experience fewer detours and roadblocks.

How Do Brain Gym Exercises Work?

Brain Gym exercises have been developed by Dennison (see p. 128), among others (Dennison 2004, Dennison/Dennison 2006 a, b, c, Teplitz 2004), in order to activate the body and mind of people trying to learn a new skill (aspect of lateralness), to relieve them (aspect of focus), and to relax them (aspect of centeredness). The exercises can help prevent learning difficulties and are of fundamental importance to learning new movements since their three characteristic aspects create the perfect learning conditions I mentioned earlier, ensuring quick progress and the satisfaction related to success.

The human brain is three-dimensionally structured and consists of parts working together as a team. It is divided into a left and a right hemisphere (aspect of lateralness), fore- and

Photo 125 *Heike demonstrates the Thymus Tapping exercise (see p. 133).*

(see p. 133)

The Brain Gym:
- Develops cross-coordination.
- Increases concentration.
- Provides a holistic approach to the rider's body.

126

hind brain (aspect of focus), and the brainstem and cerebellum (aspect of centeredness). By stimulating the different brain areas, Brain Gym exercises increase the rider's learning abilities. They also lead to a better basic attitude toward riding (important to Phase One of the Rider Training Scale—see p. 105) and build a foundation for learning with higher sensitivity.

Lateralness describes the ability to cross your brain "midline" and to activate your brain's center. Without lateralness, you can confuse your brain and develop learning disabilities. The movements required by the Brain Gym exercises support lateral integration—that is, your spatial orientation to the left will be equally good to the right. This ability is important to riders of all disciplines.

Focus is the ability to work across the line dividing your forebrain from your hind brain. There are certain reflexes that obstruct this ability. In affected riders, this leads to lack of concentration and difficulty understanding tasks as explained by an instructor, resulting in overeagerness in their efforts.

Centeredness denotes the ability to cross the line between emotion and rationality. When they do not work hand-in-hand, you will have a hard time learning.

As riding demands above-average coordination skills, the exercises included here should become second nature to you—do them not only when you feel stressed out and are presented with unfamiliar tasks, but on a daily basis (like brushing your teeth). In the end you will be able to apply your skills in a way that prevents many riding-related problems before they even arise.

Photo 126 *Brain Gym exercises for the eyes while riding at the walk improve cross-coordination.*

Exercises for Phase One: Familiarization

Note: I recommended many of these exercises in your workout on the ground, beginning on p. 25. Now I'll review them for your workout in the saddle. Refer back to Part One if more detailed instructions are needed.

Lower Stress and Promote Relaxation

Humming
Quiet humming ensures that your body's vibrations are well-calibrated. As I mentioned in Part One of this book, vibrations constantly flow through every person's body. When we are stressed, they are too high and we shake. When the vibrations

Humming—Goals:
▸ Develop positive autologous vibrations.
▸ Reactivate motion patterns that are missing/blocked.

are too low, we tend to become apathetic and stop acting or reacting. When the vibrations are just right, we are balanced.

Humming as you ride can reactivate subconscious movement patterns when you "freeze," and can shield you from outside stressors (photo 127).

127

128

Tongue-to-Palate

Push the tip of your tongue against your palate about one-fifth of an inch behind the incisors as you ride (photo 128). The exercise helps your body maintain its energy; it ensures all energy is centered. In critical life situations and during riding, you should always pay attention to the tongue's function. Its position contributes to your balance and should be considered a contributing factor when trying to achieve a sensitive seat. I provide an exercise on the ground to help demonstrate the tongue's effect on p. 25.

Tongue-to-Palate—Goal:
▸ Increase internal and external balance.

Tapping the Breastbone

As you ride, tapping your knuckles against your breastbone a couple of times reflexively activates the thymus (photo 129). I find this relieves stress, protects you from succumbing to anxiety in stressful situations, and helps establish the basis for a riding style based on "feel."

Smiling

Smiling can be a positive way to support your performance in the saddle (photo 130). When you smile, muscle chains are activated that run from your face through the back of the neck area, through the pelvis, and all the way down into the feet. I find that a rider who is smiling is more likely to be following her horse's movements.

Many riders ride with their teeth clenched, and you can clearly see how tense their masseters (muscles of mastication) are (photo 131). When the temporomandibular joint (TMJ) is "blocked," tension will spread by way of muscle chains from head, to neck, to chest, and finally, to the pelvis. Supple riding "in the moment" becomes impossible. Remember, since pelvis and head, or head and pelvis, always correspond with each other, riders who clench their teeth become involuntarily stiff.

Tapping the Breast-bone—Goals:
▸ Relieve stress.
▸ Activate autologous energy.

Smiling—Goals:
▸ Support transfer of movement within the rider.
▸ Integrate rider's and horse's rhythm.
▸ Improve relaxation and suppleness in the rider.

Try this: Clench your teeth, pressing your lower and upper jaws tightly together, and then try and shake your head. Now, open your mouth slightly and shake your head once again. You will notice that it is easier to shake your head when your jaw is not locked. By relaxing the TMJ with a smile, you can achieve a more general relaxation. Those who go through life all grim and with their teeth clenched will experience consistent TMJ pain.

Generally, we tend to take riding all too seriously and structure riding sessions too rigidly. A too serious rider can never be relaxed or supple. For this reason, riding sessions—whether lessons or training time on your own—should be designed in a way that allows for fun and occasional displays of emotion, despite the fact that riding theory needs to be seriously applied.

Positive Thoughts

Think positive. Besides smiling, pleasant thoughts and feelings have beneficial effects on the quality of your seat. Only if you are relaxed and supple can you and your horse can be balanced. This balanced state of being is the only way to develop a sensitive style of riding.

Positive Thoughts—Goals:
- Improve balance.
- Increase internal and external relaxation.
- Support transfer of movement within the rider.

Let Your Eyes Wander—Goals:

▸ Improve coordination throughout the entire body.
▸ Increase vibrations within the rider's body.
▸ Increase relaxation and suppleness.

Let Your Eyes Wander

Let your eyes wander since they determine the direction in which the rest of your body will move: The eyes lead, head and body follow suit (photos 132 & 133). This constitutes a piece of kinetic wisdom. If your eyes are staring fixedly straight ahead, your head and neck will lock and transfer this tension to your pelvis. Consequently, you will not be able to adapt to and smoothly follow your horse's movements.

This is why the terms "concentrate" and "focus" have to be approached with caution. They are commands that lead to purely intellectual reactions in the rider's left cerebral hemisphere, which is in charge of cognitive processes yet incapable of doing more than one thing at a time. If your instructor asks you to "focus," you will stare straight ahead, and as explained above, block movement through your entire body.

In the sense of athletic motion sequences, this form of focus is a questionable talent (Gallwey 1991). As a rider, you of course are expected to focus on specific tasks, and your instructor should guide you by appealing to more of your senses than just your hearing. For example, optical orientation—cones, ground poles, and the like—can be used to mark arena figures.

Controlled Breathing

Rule number one: Breathe in through your nose and out through slightly pursed lips (photos 134 & 135). Make sure you breathe out completely (in order to rid your body of all toxins) before breathing in again.

Natural human breathing is usually shallow and short and can be divided into two types: upper chest breathing and belly breathing. Most people believe that an elevated chest and sticking out your stomach are signs of good breathing technique. Both ways are wrong, however. People who breathe like this cannot fully profit from the positive effects of the air they are taking in.

The most effective way of breathing is letting the air flow into the lower and lateral parts of your chest (lower chest breathing). "Tuck in" your belly button a little so that the air can extend the sides and back of your rib cage. When you breathe in, your abdominal muscles will develop a certain amount of basic tension, which supports an upright posture. Correct breathing technique also allows your pelvis to move

**Controlled Breathing—
Goals:**
▸ Increase relaxation and
suppleness.
▸ Unify vibrations in horse
and rider.
▸ Prevent disruption of the
horse's movement during
transitions.

naturally when you are sitting on your horse; the muscles in
your pelvis area flex and relax rhythmically.

Note: When "tucking in" your belly button while breathing, do so very subtly because, eventually, you can and will
want to ask your horse to transition from one gait to another
just by doing this movement. Exaggerating the belly button
tuck increases the effect of your pelvis by restricting its back-
and-forth movement, and this sends an impulse to your horse
that he will interpret as a signal to transition. Many riders
actually briefly halt the movement of their pelvis by way of tension created in their abdominal and gluteal muscles when they
want to transition. However, this technique is often too strong
and disturbs the horse's flow of motion, leading to tension in
his body.

Gymnastics to Train Your Brain

Note: You may need an assistant to hold your horse during
these mounted exercises.

Cross-Body Movements

While in the saddle, move your left hand in the direction of
your right foot, and your right hand in the direction of your
left foot, alternating side to side (photo 136). Your eyes should
follow the direction of your hand's movement. Each hand
should travel to the opposite foot several times, crossing your

**Cross-Body
Movements—Goals:**
▸ Increase eye movement to
the left and right.
▸ Improve three-dimensional
vision in both eyes.
▸ Improve cross-
coordination.
▸ Improve spatial awareness.
▸ Support breathing and
general fitness through
movement efficiency.

body midline (the line that vertically divides your body from head to toe). This exercise requires oppositional torque.

Next, rotate your upper body and reach back to touch your horse' croup with your left hand, and then your right, crossing your body midline and alternating between left and right several times (photo 137).

Lazy Eights

While mounted, focus on a point directly in front of you at eye level. Imagine this point to be the center of a horizontal figure eight. Stretch one arm out in front of your body in a comfortable manner (you can support it with your opposite hand if needed—see fig. 113), and begin "writing" horizontal figure eights in space (photos 138 and 139). You decide on the height and width of the eights, but the best result is achieved when they are large enough to cover your entire field of vision and to make you use the full mobility of your arm.

In order to immediately stimulate the right cerebral hemisphere, start with your left arm pointing at your focal point and then move it counterclockwise to top left before returning it in a smooth circular motion back to the center. Continue the movement to the top right corner of your field of vision and in a circle again back to center. Repeat the exercise several times and with both arms. Your head (your eyes) should follow the movement to a slight degree while your neck remains relaxed. You can also do this exercise with your eyes closed and while humming (see p. 131).

Figure 113 *During the Lazy Eight exercise, you can use one hand to stabilize the opposite arm, which is extended before you.*

Lazy Eights—Goals:
- Involve both left and right cerebral hemispheres.
- Improve spatial, three-dimensional, and peripheral (at the edges of your field of view) vision, eye mobility, and coordination.
- Relax eyes, back of neck, and shoulders as your arms cross your body midline.

Elephant

While mounted, stretch your right arm in front of your body. Rest your right ear on your right upper arm and focus your eyes on the outstretched index finger of your right hand. Move your arm in the shape of horizontal figure eights while smoothly following the motion with the rest of your body (photo 140). Begin the figure eight at the part of the arch that continues to the upper right. Repeat 10 times and switch to your left arm.

Simultaneous Signs

This mounted exercise engages both cerebral hemispheres. It should be executed close to your body midline. Once you have developed a feeling for differentiating between left and right, you can do the signs along the center of your body. This exercise has an excellent effect on the large muscles in your arms and shoulders.

Elephant—Goals:

▸ Improve sight, hearing, and mobility of entire body.
▸ Increase mobility of head.
▸ Relax the back of the neck during episodes of concentration.
▸ Improve spatial and three-dimensional vision, balance (stimulates inner ear and vestibular organ), and up per and lower body coordi-nation (motion transfer).

Start by drawing symbols of your choice in the air—shapes, squiggles, jagged lines (photo 141). After a few tries, your instructor can give you specific signs to illustrate. Either way, experimenting and inventing are supposed to be at the center of this exercise. The most important aspect is to really "draw" simultaneous signs, using both the left and right hands to trace the same pattern, albeit in two different fields of vision. Try to remain as relaxed as possible during all movements.

Simultaneous Signs—Goals:

▸ Improve hand-eye coordi-nation in different fields of vision.
▸ Improve spatial awareness.
▸ Improve visual differentia-tion, lateral awareness, peripheral sight, and sense of direction and orientation.
▸ Increase body awareness.

Brain Buttons

Brain Buttons—Goals:
- Connect left and right cerebral hemispheres.
- Improve coordination.
- Trigger positive electrical and chemical reactions.
- Increase flow of electro-magnetic energy.
- Improve lateral balance.
- Relax muscles in the back of your neck.
- Promote muscle relaxation throughout body.

As explained in Part One, I use the term "brain buttons" to describe the soft tissue directly beneath the left and right collarbones (clavicles) and to either side of your breastbone (sternum). While mounted, massage these buttons vigorously for about 20 to 30 seconds while your other hand touches your belly button (photo 142 and see p. 23 for further instructions). Switch hand positions in order to activate both cerebral hemispheres.

Massaging the buttons might be a little painful at first, but the sensitivity will vanish after a few days.

You can increase the challenge of this exercise by focusing your eyes in the following ways (without moving your head): up, down, back to nose level; diagonally from top left to bottom right; diagonally from top right to bottom left; left to right at nose level. This figure is called the "butterfly eight."

143

Balance Buttons

As I explained in Part One, the "balance buttons" are located directly above the indentation where the skull rests upon the neck (approximately one inch to the left and right of your mid-line and directly next to the mastoid process of the temporal bone). When in the saddle, press or massage the left button while touching your belly button with your right hand, and vice versa (photo 143).

Space Buttons

As you did on the ground (see p. 24), place both hands on your body's midline—one in front, the other in back. The index and middle fingers of your front hand should be placed on your upper lip, while your back hand presses your tailbone (photo 144). Switch hands to activate both cerebral hemispheres. You can also gently "massage" the buttons.

Space Buttons—Goals:
- Improve awareness of midline.
- Increase centeredness, depth perception, and visual transitions between short and remote focus.
- Improve posture: hip symmetry, head position, seat and torso.
- Increase attention span.

Earth Buttons Goals:
- Improves short and remote focus of your eyes.
- Improves ability to identify and cross the midline.
- Makes your hips symmetrical.
- Improves lower body and whole-body coordination.
- Prevents excess or nervous activity.

Earth Buttons

While in the saddle, position both hands on your body's midline—your index and middle fingers of one hand should be right underneath your lower lip while your other hand touches the upper edge of your pubic bone. Hold this position for 30 seconds (or briefly massage the "buttons" before holding it), then switch hands to activate both cerebral hemispheres. At first, look down and then up or let your eyes smoothly wander up and down. You can also briefly massage the buttons before holding the pose.

Thinking Cap Goals:
- Focuses attention.
- Improves ability to cross the midline.
- Maximizes general fitness.
- Relaxes jaw, tongue, and facial muscles.

145

Thinking Cap

While in the saddle, use both your index fingers and thumbs to gently pull and fold your ears outward (photo 145). Start at the tips and gently work your way down to the earlobes. Repeat at least three times.

Positive Points

Positive Points Goals:
- Dissolves stress and tension.
- Facilitates stress-free actions.
- Gets rid of mental blocks.

While mounted, use the tips of your fingers to gently press the protuberances of the frontal bone right above your eyes, midway between your eyebrows and hairline. Concentrate on a particular negative attitude or feeling you would like to change into a more positive frame of mind from now on. Close your eyes while related negative tension falls away from you. You can also massage these "positive points" in circular (clockwise or counterclockwise) motions while keeping your eyes open, looking right, straight ahead, and left (photos 146–148).

Exercises for Phase Two: Developing Pushing Power

Schooling Balance and Rhythm on the Longe Line

A note before you begin: Commonly recommended and used exercises on the longe line often force riders into a one-size-fits-all mold. Stretching your legs too much, for example, might actually inhibit movement in your pelvis. Riders should not be forced to position their arms as if they are holding the reins, or to pull up their toes in an effort to affect a heels-down position. When you are not holding the reins but keep your hands in the position they'd be in if you were, you are, for the most part, using completely different muscles than you would if you actually had gentle contact with your horse's mouth. And pulling up your toes causes your entire leg to become stiff—you will no longer sit "still." The gentle contact between foot and stirrup suffices to place toes and heels in the naturally correct position. Deliberately pulling up your toes without the assistance of stirrups blocks movement in your legs. When riding on the longe line (or off it) without stirrups, your legs should be allowed to hang down naturally.

I feel the idea that formal exercises on the longe line without reins or stirrups will improve your seat is possibly overrated. According to function theory as part of the body mechanics approach studied by U. Göhner, changes in motion patterns can only be achieved if the same positional and energetic processes are going on inside a person as they would in the original situation that demands change. This is not the case when you are riding without reins and stirrups. (Although despite this fact, riders do experience increased mobility after they have been riding without stirrups.) On the pages that follow, you will see the riders pictured often maintain both rein and stirrup contact during longeing exercises.

▸ Your kinesthetic sense is developed through correct technique (aid application)!

Contrasting Exercises on the Longe Line

Contrasting exercises (opposites) allow you to sense and discover the position that suits you best in any given riding situation. This type of exercise can be done at the walk, trot, and canter, and requires you to take on "extreme" positions in the saddle. Assume your usual position in the saddle, then tilt your upper body as far forward as you can, as far back as you can, and to the left and right to such an extent that you just about lose your balance (photos 149–152). The extreme challenge of these different positions allows you to more easily discover perfect posture afterward—your body will be grateful when it can return to a place that is familiar as a rider and comfortable for your current physique.

▶ Assuming "extreme" and varied positions in the saddle sensitizes riders.

► Motion should flow smoothly through the entire body.

Monkey Pose on the Longe Line

Practicing "monkey pose" (forward seat—see its use on the ground on p. 84) with your head held up and tilted slightly backward (in order to free the atlanto-occipital joint) leads to a flexible dressage seat, as monkey pose creates perfect conditions for all joints. The flow of motion from head to toe becomes smoother so that the stiff rider becomes more elastic and the "loosely seated" rider is more collected and coordinated. It should be practiced at the walk, trot, and canter (photos 153–155).

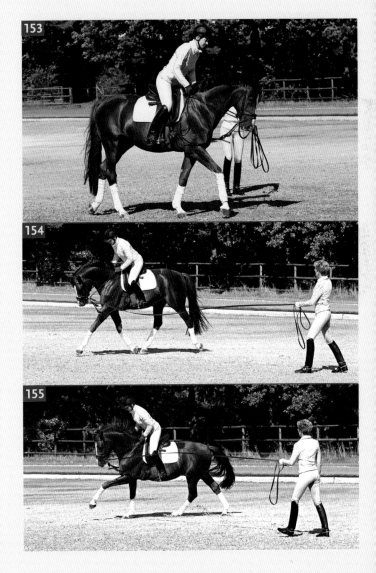

Developing Body Awareness and "Feel" on the Longe Line

Beneficial seat-improvement exercises on the longe line include almost all of the exercises described in my 6-Point Program on pp. 154–169. Practice them at the walk, trot, and canter before taking a minute to listen to your body and look for changes in the way you move and feel. In this way, you become more aware of differences in your own motion sequences.

Photo 156 *A rider demonstrates the wrap–unwrap exercise on the longe line.*

Your riding technique can only improve if you are able to feel what is going on inside you, and if you recognize and are able to give feedback related to changes in your horse's movements. This means that you have experienced and seen in your "mind's eye" the connection between (and interwovenness of) experiencing your own body and "feeling" your horse. Only if you fulfill this prerequisite will you be able to reciprocate this "information" with your aids (riding technique).

The following longe line exercises are designed to benefit both the beginner just learning to ride and also the more advanced rider who would like to develop specific aspects of awareness. On the longe line, you can fully concentrate on yourself, listen to your body, and also be made aware of changes in your body and your horse's by your instructor when you are not yet able to recognize them yourself.

On the longe line, you have the option to ask your instructor to put you in unfamiliar situations where your equestrian and perceptional development is challenged. In this context, exercises can include changes in gaits and speed by way of frequent transitions, changes of rein, tempo changes within a gait, and changes in the horse's degree of extension and collection. At a later stage of your riding training you can execute the same exercises without the assistance of the longe line. You will need to be proficient in the basic application of the different aids (weight, leg, and rein) before doing so.

When you are unable to feel what is going on underneath you and how your horse is moving, you are not able to apply correct weight, leg, and rein aids. Only after you are aware of your horse's motion patterns, will you "allow" him to move you, and as a result, use your weight, leg, and rein aids to support your horse's pushing power—instead of restricting his movements. The following exercises will help you experience your horse's movements more consciously until you have internalized them and the way they feel. I recommend you do the exercises with your eyes closed so you are not optically distracted and to help you direct your focus inward.

▶ If you know—and are able to feel—how your horse moves, you can apply the right aids at the right time.

Leaning Forward

With your eyes closed, lean forward onto your horse's neck and touch both sides of his chest with your hands (photo 157). Concentrate on when the left or right front leg, respectively, moves forward.

157

Leaning Forward and Sensing Footfalls

In the same position as in the previous exercise, this time try to tell which hind leg moves forward, and when. If you have a hard time sensing this at first, your instructor can help by telling you when your horse lifts his left or right hind leg. This makes it easier for you to perceive motion more consciously and will eventually enable you to identify motion sequences on your own.

Sensing Footfalls—Walk

Ride your horse in your natural position at the walk and follow his sequence of footfalls (with your eyes closed, if you can). First, name out loud the motion of the front legs, then the hind legs, and afterward, try to sense the sequence as a whole. In order to do this, it can help to assign numbers to the legs: left front becomes number "1," right hind is "2," right front is "3," and left hind "4."

Sensing Footfall Sequences—Trot

Determine when the left/right front leg and left/right hind leg diagonal pairs touch the ground or are lifted.

Sensing Footfall Sequences—Canter

Determine when the inside/outside hind leg leaves the ground.

The possibilities of varying the footfall sensing exercises are limitless. The goal is always to try and become aware of your horse's movements. Only if you are 100 percent sure about how your horse moves, and when, will you be able to influence it.

Exercises for Phase Three: Developing Carrying Power

The Rider's Seat and Its Motion Structure

Structure is defined as a coherent or strictly composed combination or arrangement of elements—in this case forces or motion sequences. Your seat (posture) is to be understood as a coherent and interwoven framework in which every single part has meaning and purpose.

Photo 158 *The famous invisible vertical line "running through" the rider's shoulder, hip, and foot is for purposes of general position orientation and should not be considered a strict rule.*

First of all, look at the rider as a whole: Riding posture should arrange the individual body parts in a way that would enable you to remain standing on the ground if someone were to suddenly remove your horse from under you. This means the shoulder, hip, and foot are aligned along a vertical.

This means that the so-called "chair seat" (sitting back with your feet in front of you) is just as questionable as a "fork seat" (sitting too far forward with your weight on the inside of your thighs). It is important, however, that you sit in the basic shoulder-hip-foot-in-one-line-position because it feels natural and comfortable to you and not because you or your instructor is forcing you to "hold" your body in place.

The Importance of Coordinative Interrelations within the Rider's Body

Your individual body parts are mutually dependent via the different ways they are connected. For example, the head is in charge of controlling the entire body. If it is not in its optimal position, problems result in different areas. The nose should be positioned a little more than an inch below the horizontal in order for the head to have its full mobility. If your eyes are focused lower or if your head is tilted backward, your entire body will become stiff and will no longer "follow" your horse's movements.

▶ The rider's seat is a coherent and interwoven framework.

▸Ultimately, the details of the rider's seat are not as important as the interwoven quality of the entire system.

Another example of body interdependency is the connection between the shoulders and pelvis. When your pelvis is askew, your shoulders will most likely show asymmetries, as well. When you have a humpback, it not only affects your upper body but also your pelvis, which tilts backward and forces you into a chair seat. And to go even further, a head that is positioned too far back results in a hollow back, while a head held too far forward tilts the pelvis forward. Since the head and pelvis are closely interdependent, another way to deny your pelvis flexibility is to keep your head in a stiff position, while if you allow your head to nod slightly, it has a positive effect on pelvis flexibility. And vice versa—every movement of the pelvis is mirrored by your head, albeit to a lesser degree.

The way you hold the reins and the mobility of your pelvis are also closely connected. If you mostly pull on the reins, you "block" your own pelvis; you can no longer follow your horse's movements, and your stiffly moving pelvis will disrupt your horse's motion patterns.

Photos 159 & 160 Counter-rotations of the arms is a great way to promote interdependence.

When you use your adductors (long muscles in the thighs) to drive your horse forward instead of your knee flexors (group of muscles that cross the knee joint and control joint flexion),

you become tense and inflexible. This is always the case when your toes are pointing "in" too far, toward the horse's stomach. The adductors also "block" the pelvis and keep you from following your horse's movements. And, when the muscles around your breastbone are tight or inflexible, your body will not allow the movement caused by your horse's back to flow from your pelvis up to your head—it will stop in the area of your breastbone.

As you can see, motion does not always originate in the place we discover it. The same principle holds true for incorrect movements—the causes are never where we see them. Unfortunately, instructors often make the mistake of trying to fix the symptom instead of the cause, which is why rider improvement can often take a very long time.

Remember, looking at your body parts in an isolated manner does not tell you much about the structure or system as a whole. It is the interactions between the individual parts and their interdependencies that are important. For this reason, one shouldn't look for details in a rider's posture when first "judging" her, but instead should get a sense of the "big picture."

Coordinated motion is defined as the organization of individual submovements that work together and depend on each other for achieving a common goal. Subactions are coordinated (linked together and structured) in a way that creates the execution of the main action. Coordinated motion is exposed to many negative internal (rider) and external (horse) forces, which make it difficult to achieve. For example:

▸ Mental issues, such as stress (see p. 25).
▸ Lack of mobility in your joints, including the atlanto-occipital joint, sacroiliac joints, shoulders, elbows, hands, hips, knees, and feet.
▸ Lack of flexibility in the breastbone and/or pelvic area.
▸ Overly strong reflexes.
▸ Lack of ability to rotate left and right.
▸ Insufficient quality of motion in the horse.
▸ Differences in "vibrations" of horse and rider.
▸ Unfavorable difference in body height proportions between horse and rider.
▸ Change of conditions (mostly external forces that affect horse and rider)—for example, noise/sounds, soft/hard ground, rain, wind, spectators.

▸ Focus on the complete system first, and the details of your seat second.

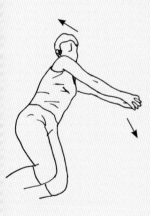

Figure 114 *Some exercises dealing with cross-coordination need to be practiced on the ground before they can be applied on horseback (see Part One, p. 84, for exercises on the ground).*

The 6-Point Program on Horseback

As I explained in Part One, my so-called 6-Point Program (see p. 15) was developed upon the request of riding instructors who were looking for a practical program that would help them, help their students quickly change and improve their seat. I've chosen six focus areas (to simplify, I call them "points" although I acknowledge they do not all qualify as a defined region of the human body) in order to form a basic structure a rider's training can follow. The six points can be addressed in any order, depending on a rider's particular problems. All six are connected to each other in one way or another.

Since the six points are interchangeable, they consequently pertain to different steps of the Rider's Training Scale (see p. 105). They are the logical result of analyzing the structure of the rider's seat, which consists of six central areas.

▶ The 6-Point Program provides a structure for improving a rider's seat in no time.

In the Saddle vs. on the Ground—Differences in the 6-Point Program

When you massage the atlanto-occipital joint or the back of your skull, for example, you not only influence the area of your neck, you also change the position of your pelvis, and in doing so your ankles will start to absorb movement like springs. Mobilizing the breastbone area usually has positive effects on your shoulders so that the "rotational seat" (see p. 84) riding requires on circles and turns comes more naturally to you, and you can use the reins more gently.

Since Part Two of this book requires you to remain in the saddle, I have made slight changes to the basic structure of the 6-Point Program you did on the ground in Part One (see p. 15). For example, one exercise to "unlock" (mobilize) the sacroiliac joints cannot be done on horseback. The mobility of these joints can only be achieved in the saddle through flexibility exercises targeting the pelvis and other joints. For this reason, they are combined in this section.

▶ The head leads; the body follows.

In addition, in the saddle we address all the major joints rather than focusing on the pelvis. It is important to work your way through them, from head to toe, in order to facilitate transfer and flow of motion. This kind of functionality can be achieved on horseback by making sure all joint systems are working well, thus creating perfect conditions to allow motion and energy to flow through your body—for the most part uninterruptedly.

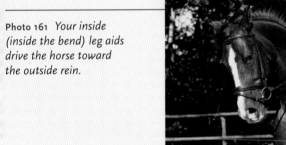

▸ Joints facilitate the flow of motion from head to toe, and vice versa.

On another note, when in the saddle, the forward-driving aids cannot be improved by doing knee flexor exercises such as those described in Part One (see p. 45), as the movements related to the exercises might confuse the horse. Sitting astride a chair or sawhorse is a good way to practice "pushing the right buttons" and using your muscles correctly, and your instructor can also place her hands underneath your calves and ask you to demonstrate how you apply the aids so she can then help guide you. Unfortunately, it is impossible to teach a student on a horse how to time the aids and vary them in intensity, so instructors must instead resort to improving cross-coordination as a way to help develop a "feel" for correct application of the forward-driving leg aids.

▸ Forward-driving leg aids are connected to rein contact and cross-coordination.

Forward-driving leg aids always cause diagonal motion transfer throughout the horse's body—for example, your inside leg (inside the bend) drives the horse toward the outside rein. In this way, using your forward-driving aids is simultaneously connected to the cross-coordination necessary in handling the reins.

Photo 161 *Your inside (inside the bend) leg aids drive the horse toward the outside rein.*

The 6-Point Program in the Saddle

Head and neck are

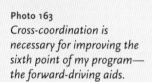

Sacroiliac joint(s)
pelvic mobility

5

Mobility of major
joints

163

Photo 163
*Cross-coordination is
necessary for improving the
sixth point of my program—
the forward-driving aids.*

Breastbone and ribcage

Muscle and tendon reflexes

6

Forward-driving aids

Photo 164 *Mobilizing the head and neck area will help you ride better.*

▶ The atlanto-occipital joint ensures vibrations (see p. 15) can travel through your entire body.

▶ Unrestricted mobility of the atlanto-occipital joint is fundamental to good riding.

POINT 1:

The Head and Neck Area

Your head has superior control over the rest of your body— that is, the head "leads" and the body "follows." Unfortunately, most people struggle with this natural physical inclination because their head and neck areas are not correctly positioned. It all starts with the masseters (the "chewing" muscles along your jaw): If you work them too hard, they tense up and restrict the lateral rotation of your head and—as discussed—this can even affect the mobility of your pelvis. You will then have a hard time adapting to your horse's movements because your seat has become inflexible.

The atlanto-occipital joint and the skull have an even greater influence on your ability to smoothly follow your horse's movements and rotate your body in the saddle. The atlanto-occipital joint marks the transition from skull to first cervical vertebra and needs to move freely. If this joint is restricted, all other joints lose their mobility to some degree, and your body will not allow movements to smoothly flow through its

▸ Ribcage mobility facilitates the passage of vibrations from pelvis to head, and vice versa.

entire length. As discussed earlier in this book, the atlanto-occipital joint can only move freely if your eyes are pointing straight ahead and slightly downward.

Many riders experience negative tension in the muscles around their skull because in everyday life, they rotate their head in the wrong way. You have to "unlock" your atlanto-occipital joint and reduce the tension around your skull in order to execute rotational movements smoothly and efficiently and allow vibrations (from your body and your horse's) to pass through your body from head to toe, and vice versa. Relieving strain in this area relaxes your upper body and allows your pelvis to change position in a way that leads to a more flexible seat with elastic ankles.

The seat of a rider always has to be treated in a holistic manner. Changing your head position can have positive or negative effects on your feet while, in the same way, the position of the stirrups (positioned perpendicular to and under the widest point of your feet) allows your entire body (head to toe) to absorb the horse's movements. If the stirrup is placed too close to the tips of your toes or your heels, all motion transmission within your body is obstructed. Furthermore, pressing your heels down or pulling them up in a misguided attempt to drive your horse forward restricts the mobility of your body all the way up into your head.

POINT 2:
Breastbone and Rib Cage

When riding a horse, the vibrations of his movements are meant to flow from your pelvis up to your head; however, they are often "stopped" in the thoracic spine. This part of the human body is much less flexible than, for example, the cervical or lumbar spine, as the rib cage acts like a relatively stiff "corset." For this reason, many riders experience pain in this area when they have to ride sitting trot. If a person has a stiff pelvis on top of that, all her movements will be bumpy or jerky. Since the ribs restrict the flexibility of the thoracic spine, you need to pay special attention to mobilizing this area.

POINT 3:
Muscle and Tendon Reflexes

Stress translates into high negative tension in various muscles and tendons. Stretching does not help in this case; however, if

165

Photo 165 *Heike Kemmer demonstrates how to stimulate the tendons of the knee from the saddle: Place your fingers underneath where your thighs and knees merge. You will feel two tendons left and right of your knee—gently "pinch" or "pluck" them.*

you "pluck" or "pinch" your trapezius muscles, pectoralis, adductors, psoas major, abdominal obliques, biceps, and triceps (for example), you can ease tension. Addressing the adductor and psoas muscles, especially, will allow you to sit deeper in the saddle and help your pelvis follow your horse's motion.

In the beginning, the pinches might feel unpleasant, which only underlines the significance of the problem. But if you repeat the exercises every day, you will feel significantly better after only a few days.

POINT 4:
The Sacroiliac Joint and Pelvic Mobility

Even if all your muscles are evenly developed and work in harmony, you will not be able to "follow" your horse's movements if your sacroiliac joints are "blocked." Most forms of back problems actually originate in this joint. It is significant in the human body because it both allows for or obstructs our natural motion patterns, which are all three-dimensional (back-forth, left-right, up-down).

According to the Feldenkrais Method, which is designed to improve movement and reduce pain or limitations related to it, the pelvis is, so to speak, the "engine" of the human body—it absorbs and emits energy, acting as a "transmission device"

Photo 166 *Heike shows how to mobilize the hip and shoulder joints.*

▸ The human body's system of joints allows for smooth motion.

that passes on all movement from legs to head, and vice versa. The rider uses it to communicate with the horse's back. Many of the back problems people complain about these days occur because they do not know how to use their pelvis correctly anymore. The pelvis needs to be able to execute three-dimensional movements as described above. Stiffness in any one direction not only causes problems for the rider, it also negatively influences the horse via his back.

POINT 5:
Mobility of Major Joints

Nowadays, our society is characterized by reduced motion (we are less active), which leads to different kinds of problems in our body. Joints are especially affected as lack of physical activity combined with monotonous or partly unnatural movements prevent their functionally correct usage. While the negative effects of this are apparent in all athletic disciplines, riders especially feel it and instructors recognize related problems based on visible negative tension in certain areas of their students' bodies. This tension disturbs integral motion sequences and, thus, interferes with communication with the horse.

The functions of atlanto-occipital and sacroiliac joints have already been mentioned (see pp. 15 and 40). In riders,

Photo 167 *Heike practices slow, circular motions with her arms.*

additional problems arise in the shoulders, wrists, hips, knees and feet.

Shoulder joints: The shoulder joint is basically a ball and socket joint whose true purpose is neglected. Even though the joint is constructed in a way that allows for movements in all directions, our "daily grind" and subsequent lack of motion do not use it to its full potential. The less frequently the body is being used, and the less variety in its uses, the faster it becomes inflexible.

Due to (computer-based) working conditions, people tend to pull up their shoulders while working in a seated position (in addition to other issues with the head and neck area). High levels of stress in our daily life reinforce this "pulled-up" position even more. Because of the lack of full usage of the shoulder joints, your arms do not hang in a relaxed manner from your shoulders, and your entire shoulder area becomes stiff. This is evident in the saddle as it negatively affects the way you hold your hands and the reins (see more about this when I discuss the wrists below).

Inflexible hands/arms/shoulders have motion-restricting effects on the hips—hand position issues are often really pel-

▶ Unrestricted shoulder joints have a positive influence on the head and neck area and also make gentle rein contact possible.

vis posture issues, and vice versa. When you pull on the reins, the pelvis is involuntarily drawn closer to the hands. You must be able to constantly maintain a delicate contact with your horse's mouth, and apply both yielding and "asking" rein aids, for your pelvis to move independently. So again we see how the root of a problem is rarely found where you see the symptoms. If your riding instructor only focuses on your hand position, you will isolate it and think only about it—and when you concentrate too hard on it, you will use too many of the wrong muscles and become tense.

Wrists: Based on our body structure, we cannot move our muscles in isolation from each other but must employ coordinated muscle chains instead. As discussed, this phenomenon affects motion transfer between the shoulders and pelvis, but all the more between the shoulders and hands. Lack of mobility in your shoulders reveals itself in stiff hand movements.

Structurally, the wrist is a hinge joint that is equipped with an additional direction of possible motion: rotation. The motion necessary for rein aids—to yield and "ask"—using just your wrists has become more and more of a problem for modern riders because we have reduced the equalizing use of flexors and extensors in our arms to such a degree as to destroy harmony. To a greater extent, it is common to see riders

Photo 168 *Heike rotates her hands in different directions.*

▶ The wrists are in charge of finely adjusting the motion produced by the horse's hindquarters.

with downturned palms or their hands curled in. This poses a problem with respect to following the natural nodding motion of the horse's head and neck. The only way to rhythmically adjust to this nodding is to increase the scope of the rotation in the wrist, while at the same time, you have to regain the ability to rhythmically flex and stretch the muscles in your forearms. (Note: The elbows rarely pose a problem in this regard.)

Hip joints: The hip joint is the largest joint in your body and as we've discussed in this book, it is connected to a great number of muscles. Most of the movement humans are involved in today occurs on even surfaces, so the hip is used mostly as a hinge joint instead of the ball-and-socket joint it actually is. As a result, many of the surrounding muscles reduce their activity, leading to restricted function of the hip joints.

▶ Unrestricted hip joints lead to long, relaxed legs and a flexible pelvis.

If we had to move around on uneven ground all the time, the hips' abilities would not "wither" as they have. In fact, footwear with curved soles—such as the popular fitness "rocker" shoes—can help riders remain flexible in the hips, knees, and ankles, as well as the sacroiliac joints.

Photo 169 *Heike demonstrates circular motions with outstretched legs in the saddle.*

169

Inflexible hip joints lead to two fundamental weaknesses in riders: The flexibility of your pelvis is decreased and you can no longer just let your legs hang down from your hips in a relaxed manner. When you see a rider whose heels "lower" with every step her horse takes, you know that the rider's muscle chains transfer motion perfectly (knees to heels). The heels are reactive parts the motion that pulses through the rider's body. This means a command for a rider to "stretch her legs" or "push her heels down" are inappropriate or even wrong. Commands like these are counterproductive because they create actions instead of (intrinsically automatic) reactions.

▸ When your knees are relaxed you have fewer problems with your forward-driving aids.

Knee joints: The knee joint works as a hinge joint and is an important juncture between the hips and feet. Unfortunately, as a society we sit for most of the day, which causes the flexors and extensors in our thighs and calves to become short and tight. As a result, tendons located in these areas (patellar, hamstring, and Achilles tendons) are exposed to increased pressure, which inhibits the flexing and stretching (motion transfer from feet, to pelvis, to upper body and back) required during rising trot, sitting trot, and canter. It is possible to stimulate the muscles and tendons of the knee in order to turn the knee joint back into the "motion transfer joint" it actually is and get it to allow the required flow of motion from upper body to feet.

Ankles: The ankles can be an obstacle to smooth, seamless riding because they often do not allow the heels to lower elastically. The roots of the problem lie in decreased flexibility of the pelvis and the knee joints, shortened calf muscles, tension in the Achilles tendon, and one-sided use of the ankles. When we walk, we use our ankles mostly to stretch. When I ask riders to stretch and to flex their toes several times, they often run into trouble with regard to their tibialis anterior muscles (the muscles that act to dorsiflex and invert the foot), which get overwhelmed as they tend to be weak as opposed to the often shortened calf muscles. Ideally, the ankles operate functionally within the chain of motion of hip/knee/ankle and allow for motion; varied exercises may be necessary in order to regain flexibility in this area.

▸ Flexible ankles allow for "cushioning" motion within your body with every step your horse takes.

Integration of all joints: Improving joint mobility in an isolated manner is one thing, integrating them into motion sequences is another. Movements within the body have to be passed on (connected) in a way that makes motion flow smoothly and continuously. This means you must not feel or see any "edges," "rough patches," or other forms of "interference" within a motion sequence that spans your body from head to feet, and vice versa. Integration of joint mobility can be achieved by practicing "monkey pose" (see pp. 84 and 147).

Motion transfer from pelvis to head, or pelvis to feet can only happen if none of the important joints involved (ankles, knees, hips, shoulders, wrists, and atlanto-occipital joint) disrupts transfer and flow of motion within the rider's body. Mobilizing the joints connects individual body parts more easily and leads to simultaneous and successive interconnections between them. For example, as we discussed in Part One, flexible ankles and heels can be achieved by stimulating ("pinching" or "plucking") the Achilles tendon, but their elasticity mostly depends on the mobility of hip and atlanto-occipital joints.

▶ All your major joints need to be understood as a system.

If some areas in your body are relaxed (mobile) while others are stiff, your body will react with countermovements (movements made in opposition to another), which have a strong negative effect on your horse. For this reason, you have to become "loose" and relaxed throughout your body so all movements feel easy and flow uninhibitedly. By coordinating all your body parts in connection with each other, you create a self-contained, stable—yet flexible—posture.

POINT 6:
Forward-Driving Aids

Many people have lost their cross-coordination skills (mobility around the midline) due to the lack of variety in the movements they have experienced from childhood to adulthood. Children, for the most part, learn to crawl before they learn how to walk. The crawling motion is a reflex (Amphibian Reflex) and basically tied to humans and their natural development.

▶ Being flexible around and across your midline allows you to apply effective forward-driving aids and fine-tune your rein aids.

Since children now face restrictions in the ways they can move and exercise, genetically defined patterns are no longer developed, which has serious negative effects on learning processes in general (such as writing and math) and motion processes in particular.

170

Photo 170 *Cross-coordinated movement is necessary for subtle and efficient forward-driving aids.*

Riders, however, constantly need the basic motion patterns we relied on as children, so we have to redevelop/relearn them, which requires great effort and energy in most cases.

The sooner the processes are reactivated, the easier it is to learn how to ride. This includes developing the "rotational seat" (see p. 84), a natural movement during which the shoulders move in the opposite direction of the pelvis without your thinking about it. This movement needs to be restored in your subconscious with the help of specific exercises. Once relearned, it will help you sit in a natural way with your shoulders parallel to your horse's shoulders, and your pelvis parallel to his, as well. This way, you are sitting "in" your horse's movements—that is, you assimilate.

As already mentioned in the section on cross-coordinative exercises (see pp. 21 and 136), these exercises are target preparation for the rider's "rotational seat" and especially designed for those who have not yet mastered it. If you cannot rotate your shoulders in the opposite direction of your pelvis, you will never assimilate to your horse's rhythm and will not learn to "feel" his movements. Your seat is not stable or self-contained, which makes it impossible to "follow" your horse's

▶ Correctly applied forward-
driving aids are applied
using the hamstrings.

motion. The exercises I've provided in this book physically and mentally prepare you to forget about the rotating movement; only then can you internalize the process so it happens automatically and in reaction to particular situations, as needed.

Because you cannot prepare for the use of forward-driving aids when you are sitting on your horse in the same way as we did on the ground, there will not be specific exercises in this section; however, as mentioned, the forward-driving aids are directly related to cross-coordination (diagonal aids such as inside leg, outside rein).

Your instructor can help teach you the direction and form of the quick impulse you need to apply, and he or she can help you in a tactile way by positioning a hand between your calf and the horse's body in order to feel your aids. You can also feel your hamstrings at work by placing your own hand underneath your thigh. While applying the aids, your toes need to point slightly away from the horse (left and right feet pointing to eleven and one o'clock, respectively) in order to ensure the correct direction of your calf movement. The calves have to

Photo 171 *I show Heike how to correctly apply the forward-driving aids.*

act in the blink of an eye without being "pressed" against the horse's body. You also have to avoid turning your calves out while pinching with your knees and using the adductors in your thighs to drive the horse forward.

▶ The rider's toes should
point slightly outward.

When you start learning correct aid application, your brain will need big impulses in order to learn or relearn—for example, at first you have to exaggerate the "swinging" motion (stretching) of your calf in order to make sure that the hamstrings are well extended. Over time, the exaggerated movements should decrease significantly and become progressively quicker, eventually turning into the subtle impulse aids are meant to be.

The 6-Point Program in the Saddle

Many of the exercises that follow are much the same as those you did on the ground in Part One. Please refer back for more information or clarification.

Point 1: The Head and Neck Area

Head Rotations

Move your head in different directions—forward and back, left and right, pull it down between your shoulders and stretch it up "tall" (photos 172 & 173). Repeat several times. Try not to go in the same direction twice; you want to explore all possible head positions. Use your imagination.

▶ Try to move your head in 20 to 30 different ways.

"Head Shake"

In the saddle, sit so you feel your seat bones (ischium). Relax your arms and let them hang down by your sides. Using quick and very subtle movements (one-half to one inch only), turn

your head from left to right. The muscles in your head and neck should not tense up; instead, they are supposed to "exercise" as effortlessly as possible. Continue "shaking" for about one minute, then turn your head slightly to your left and repeat the "head shake" exercises. Repeat to the right side.

Head and Eyes in Opposite Directions

While on your horse, turn your head from left to right while moving your eyes in the opposite direction (photo 174). Repeat 10 times in both directions.

Massage and Stretch the Atlanto-Occipital Joint

It is possible to relieve tension in the area around the atlanto-occipital joint by doing the following massage exercise while you're in the saddle: Using the ring, middle, and index fingers of both hands, massage the point where your skull and uppermost cervical vertebra meet (photos 175 & 176). Afterward, you may want to perform the following stretching exercise: Place the tip of your left middle finger on your atlanto-occipital joint; place the tip of your right middle finger on your left middle finger. With your elbows stretched sideways, put firm pressure on the joint.

Massage Your Skull

Tension can also be relieved by massaging your skull while mounted. This area needs to be massaged slowly but intensely as it is very tight in most people due to poor rotational movements of the head. At first, you will probably experience discomfort, but it will fade away quickly if you continue the practice several times a day.

Lower Jaw, Facial Muscle and Tongue Movements

In a slow and smooth motion, slide your lower jaw from left to right as far as possible. At the same time, stretch your facial muscles in the opposite direction (photos 177 & 178). Vary the exercise by pushing your upper jaw forward and pulling it backward. Afterward, make all kinds of funny faces using your facial muscles: Purse your lips, stretch both corners of your mouth outward, and come up with other playful movements you can do with your face (photos 179 & 180). Stick your tongue out and try to touch your chin and nose, then move it from left to right as far as possible. At first, go through these motions actively. Then, use your fingers to pull

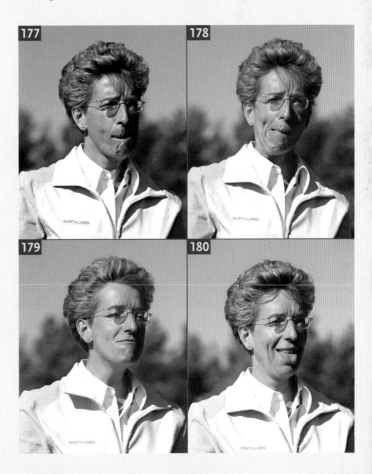

your tongue in different directions. (Note: In these instances your tongue must not move on its own; your fingers should do all the work.)

Finally, coordinate the movements of your tongue and eyes. When you look to your upper left, point your tongue toward the lower right, and vice versa. And when you look to your lower left, point your tongue toward the upper right, and vice versa.

"Monkey Pose"

I introduced you to "monkey pose" (forward seat) in the saddle on p. 84. Practice this pose on horseback every now and then (photo 181). Although forward seat is familiar to many, it is difficult for most riders to do correctly. Especially stiff riders gain suppleness when they consistently practice the monkey pose, as it encourages a high degree of mobility in all joints. You need to practice and hold monkey pose with a great deal of self-awareness or do it when your instructor is available to provide accurate feedback regarding your position.

▸ If you get tired during any of the workouts, on the ground or in the saddle, take a short break.

Practice monkey pose in walk, trot, and canter with extremely short stirrups. Lift your buttocks out of the saddle in all three gaits. (Note: Do not "sit" for a stride as you might in posting trot.) The exercise done at the three gaits unlocks all

major joints (ankles, knees, hips, and shoulders), makes stiff riders significantly more flexible, and helps atonic ("limp") riders show better form and posture.

New Motion Patterns for Your Head

Sit in the saddle with your weight evenly distributed on both seat bones. Place your right hand on your head. Your head should not move by itself—your hand controls its movements, from left to right, and only as far as possible without causing strain (photo 182). Do not attempt to work through resistance.

Switch hands. Place your left hand on your head and move your head gently from left to right. Your head again needs to give your hand full control. Repeat 8 to 12 times in each direction. The focus of these movements lies in mobilizing the muscles in your neck. You will find a variation of this exercise for the pelvis on p. 183.)

Unlocking the Back of Your Neck with Your Toes

Take your feet out of the stirrups and let your legs hang down in a relaxed manner. Move your toes in circular motions that vary in size and direction (clockwise/counterclockwise). Vary the movement as much as possible (photos 183 & 184).

Now place your feet in your stirrups and continue with circular motions of different size and intensity. Tilt your feet outward and inward so they rest on their outer or inner edge (photos 185 & 186).

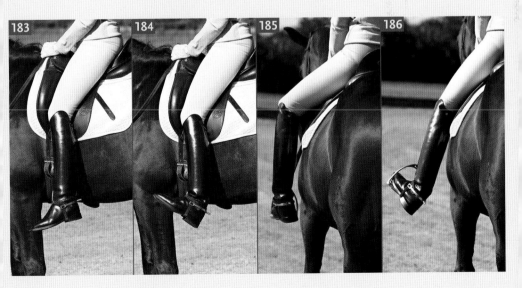

Gentle Head Movements

Perform the following movements slowly and gently (not fast and jerky): Roll your head forward, hold for a short moment, then roll your head gently to the left, and to the right. Roll your head backward, hold for a short moment, then roll your head gently to the left and right (photos 187 & 188). Repeat circular movements 3 to 5 times, both clockwise and counterclockwise. Keep breathing rhythmically during the entire exercise and stay away from extreme positions, which can cause negative tension. Keep your mouth open while rolling your head backward. You always need to feel like you can still swallow. When you come to a place where you experience tightness in your muscles, hold the pose until the tension has disappeared. You can loosen your shoulders during this exercise by performing it with both "raised" shoulders and relaxed shoulders.

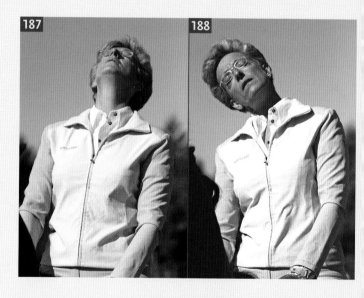

At first, practice the movements with your eyes closed. Then repeat with your eyes open. Note: Never allow your head to just "drop"; your muscles always need to stabilize it slightly.

Stretching the Back of the Neck

Always be very careful when stretching this area and proceed slowly and dynamically—not statically! It should take some time to get from your starting position to the complete stretch. Repeat each one 8 to 10 times.

Exercise 1: While seated in the saddle with your feet in stirrups and your fingers interlaced behind your head, pull your head forward and downward with your hands (photo 189).

Exercise 2: While seated in the saddle with your neck upright, use your left hand to pull your head as far sideways as possible as your right arm pushes downward toward the floor. Repeat and switch sides (photo 190).

Exercise 3: While seated in the saddle as in Exercise 2, your hand leads your forward and sideways, rather than just sideways (photo 191).

Exercise 4: While seated in the saddle with your fingers interlaced in front of your forehead, pull your head backward (photo 192).

Exercise 5: While seated in the saddle, pull your head diagonally backward and sideways (photo 193). (Note: To intensify the effect of the last five exercises, turn your chin slightly to the left and right when you reach the end position of the respective stretching move.)

Exercise 6: While seated in the saddle, bend one arm at neck level, place your other hand on your elbow, and push the arm backward.

POINT 2:
Breastbone and Rib Cage

Axial Rotation—Focus on Your Hand

> ▸ Repeat all exercises in this section from 8 to 12 times in each direction.

While in the saddle, stretch your right arm forward at shoulder level, then bend your elbow at an almost 90 degree angle and relax your wrist so your hand hangs down freely. Your hand should be about 20 inches from your face. Focus on your hand

and turn your arm as far to the left and right as possible without straining. Keep your eyes on your hand. Repeat 10 times and switch arms.

Independent Head Movements

Assume the same pose as in the previous exercise and, beginning with your right arm, turn it as far to the left as possible. Hold the pose with your eyes on your hand. Then turn only your head even further to the left before swinging your arm and head (keep your eyes on your hand) back into the starting position (photo 194). Repeat 10 times, then switch arms.

Opposite Movements: Shoulders vs. Hips

While mounted, cross your arms in front of your chest and place your hands on your shoulders. Do not actively move your shoulders but use your hands to move them, instead. With the help of your hands, turn your shoulders to the left while turning your left hip to the right, and vice versa (photo 195).

Wrap—Unwrap

In the saddle, stretch your right arm forward at shoulder level, then bend your elbow at an almost 90-degree angle, and relax your wrist so your hand hangs down freely. Your hand should be about 20 inches from your face. Move your arm to the left, toward your body, and around your head while your head is turning right ("wrapping"). Then, move your arm to the right and away from your body while turning your head to the left ("unwrapping"). Repeat with your left arm (photo 196).

Integrating Shoulders and Hip Joints

In this exercise, you move your shoulder and hip joint on one side closer to each other ("shortening" that side of your torso) and then away from each other (stretching that side of your torso) (photo 197). Repeat on both sides. (See more exercises designed for the shoulders and to mobilize the thoracic spine and upper body on pp. 79 and 152.)

Point 3: Muscle and Tendon Reflexes

Trigger Trapezius and Pectoralis Muscle Reflexes

Negative tension and stiffness in the trapezius or pectorals can be relieved through "plucking" or "pinching"—and you can do this in the saddle as well as on the ground (p. 38). Use your thumb plus your index or middle finger for the "plucking" (photos 198 & 199). Note: The pinching/plucking might be relatively unpleasant at first. The feeling will fade away once you incorporate the exercise in your daily routine.

▶ Do not apply force or use more strength than necessary.

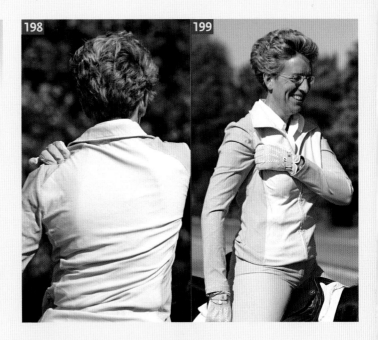

Stretching (Relaxing) the Hip Flexors

It is possible to reduce the strong reflexes that control the hip flexors (the group of skeletal muscles that move your thigh bone)—in effect, "relaxing" or stretching them. As a result, your pelvis will be better able to assimilate to your horse's movements because it will not tip forward and "lock" as much anymore.

As you learned in Part One (see p. 39), you can feel your inner hip muscles (a group collectively known as the iliopsoas muscles) when you lift your feet a little bit while sitting in the saddle. The hip flexor, as an extension of the thigh muscle, will tense up. Massage the muscle with your fingertips, rubbing from left to right (photo 200). If this feels unpleasant, start gently and slowly increasing the pressure. If attended to on a daily basis, the hip flexor will quickly become more supple.

The inner hip flexors (including the adductor) are best massaged with the "pinching"/"plucking" motion you've used in other exercises. Sit in the saddle with your legs slightly spread away from the seat. Use your thumb and index/middle fingers to press against the muscle-tendon strand and pluck at it, working your way from your knees up to your pubic bone (photo 201). What might feel uncomfortable at first will quickly improve in sensation. Note: When you first incorporate

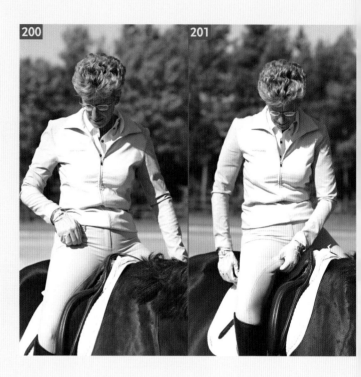

these exercises into your routine, you may experience actual sores due to myofascial adhesions. Connective tissue (fascia) within the body can become "entangled" over time, interfering with blood circulation and muscle movement, and myofascial adhesions are a result of unattended impingements. They occur due to injury, illness, inactivity, nutrition, and the aging process, among others.

Hamstring Tendon

Seated in the saddle, place your fingers underneath your thigh where the thigh meets the knee. You will feel two tendons to the left and right of your knee—"pluck" or "pinch" them several times (photo 202).

Patellar Tendon

You can stimulate the patellar tendon by applying light pressure to the point directly underneath your kneecap where you can feel a direct line into the shinbone. Use your fingertips to rub over this point from left to right (photo 203).

Lateral Core Muscles

These muscles are located between the hips and the edges of the ribs, where they help stabilize the torso during lateral compensation movements of the pelvis (too much pressure on one seat bone or a collapsed hip). The lateral core muscles often show differing degrees of tension, which can be equalized by stimulating them with massage. Sit in the saddle, and grab the muscle strand on each side of your waist with your thumb and index finger and roll it over your fingers, slightly "pinching" the muscle (photo 204).

Biceps and Triceps

When your hands tend to be too high or too low while riding, you can stimulate the biceps (flexor) and triceps (extensor) located in your upper arms by equalizing the balance of tension existing between them. With your thumb and index/middle finger, "pinch" and "pluck" at both muscle/tendon strands in order to "relax" the flexor, which is often predominant, and thus create a balance of tension between both muscle areas (photos 205 & 206).

Muscles of the Forearm

You can feel the location of the muscle-tendon strands running from your fingers to your elbow by flexing your thumb or lifting an index finger as far as you can to cause the respective muscle-tendon strand to contract. Stimulate these strands by massaging them with the tips of the fingers of your other hand, proceeding in gentle, small, back-and-forth movements (photo 207). After this exercise, your forearm will feel significantly lighter since all tension will have disappeared.

POINT 4:
Sacroiliac Joints and Pelvic Mobility

In most cases, you should repeat the following exercises from 8 to 12 times on each side.

Sitting Dynamically

Break up stereotypical (static) sitting patterns by sliding one buttock down the side of the saddle and lifting and lowering that side of your body 8 to 12 times (photo 208). Repeat on the other side. You will experience a pleasant change in your entire body structure.

Face of the Clock

As you sit on your horse, imagine yourself sitting on the face of a clock (we did a similar exercise on the ground, beginning on p. 40). When you lower your pelvis to the right, you are sitting on three o'clock. When you lower your pelvis to the left, you are sitting on nine o'clock. You can execute these two movements one after the other or combine them in one fluid motion. Vary the pace of your movements. Then, tip your pelvis forward toward twelve o'clock and backward toward six o'clock. Again combine in one fluid motion and vary the pace. Continue with circular motions in all directions, and come up with your own "times," such as moving from seven o'clock to one o'clock or two o'clock to eight o'clock. Be creative in order to increase the flexibility of your pelvis and sacroiliac joints.

Contrasting Exercises at Halt, Walk and Trot

Contrasting exercises feature multiple movements that are slow then fast, exaggerated then subtle, forward then backward, and the like. Your task is to "feel" and become aware of the differences between the motion sequences. Your horse's reactions will tell you how he receives and feels about the movements.

It is quite possible to change the way you sit in the saddle by practicing contrasting movements, such as sitting extremely to the right and then to the left, leaning far forward and then far backward (photos 209 & 210). These contrasts offer

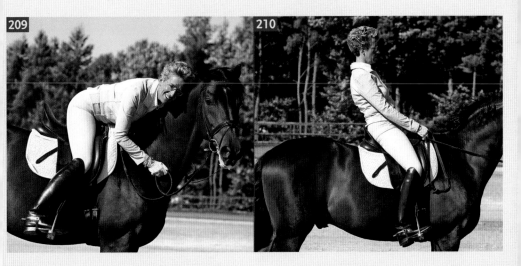

variations in position to your brain. Every person's brain still possesses the ability to find the best individual solution for a specific situation, so after varying your posture, your brain will let you know which position is most secure, stable, and harmonious.

Forcing a rider into a standardized mold we consider the "correct seat" (as often done) is usually a dead end. Though you may think you are sitting as you should, you will sit stiffly and inflexibly. Using "feel" when riding means that you and your horse become one in your movements, and while you have full control over your four-legged partner, your influence helps his natural movements "blossom."

POINT 5:
Mobility of Major Joints

Repeat each of the following exercises from 8 to 12 times on each side.

Move Your Shoulders in all Directions

While in the saddle, lift one shoulder, lower the shoulder, then combine both movements. Move your shoulder forward, move your shoulder backward, and combine the movements (photos 211 & 212). Repeat with your other shoulder. Do complete circles with your shoulders.

Shoulder Circles—Arm Outstretched

Do slow and deliberate circular movements with one arm stretched out (photo 213). The motion should be controlled. Repeat the movements with the other arm, and with both arms at the same time—circling in the same direction and in opposite directions.

Hip Joints in All Directions

Sitting in the saddle, move one of your hip joints forward, backward, and then in a fluid motion in both directions (photo 214). Move the hip up and then down, and then in a complete fluid motion. Finally, do circular motions both clockwise and counterclockwise. Repeat with your other hip.

Integrating Shoulders and Hip Joints

On one side of your body, lower your shoulder and lift your hip (shortening). Then, lift your shoulder and lower your hip (stretching). Repeat with your other side (photo 215).

Head-to-Shoulder

In the saddle, tilt your head sideways and lift the respective shoulder so head and shoulder come closer to each other

(shortening). Repeat with the other side (photo 216). Then, stretch each side by tilting your head to the left and lowering your right shoulder, and vice versa.

Head-to-Hip

Tilt your head sideways and lift the respective hip (shortening). Repeat with the other side (photo 217). Then, stretch your side by tilting your head to the left and lowering your right hip, and vice versa.

Wrists—Bending, Stretching, Twisting, Rotating

On your horse, bend one wrist in both directions, using your other hand to assist the movement (passive stretching in both directions). Why? The extent to which a body part can be passively bent (indicating flexibility) is always greater when caused by external forces (yourself or an assistant) than it is when bent actively (photo 218). Only externally generated bending actively increases the degree of passive flexibility.

Turn your forearms inward and outward, rotating your lower arm through twisting of the radius and ulna (pronation). During pronation, the radius rolls around the ulna at the wrist and the elbow (photo 219). Next, rotate your wrists clockwise and counterclockwise.

Leg Rotation

Take your feet out of the stirrups and rotate your legs clockwise and counterclockwise (photo 220). Vary the size of the

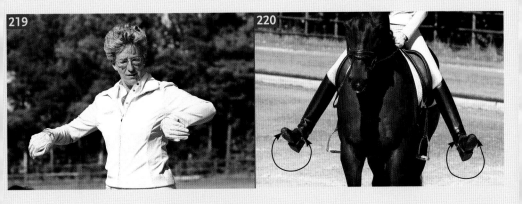

circles the entire time so all muscles connected to the hip joints are mobilized. You can add to the exercise by either stretching or bending your toes.

Cycling

Take your feet out of the stirrups and move your legs as if you were riding a bike (photos 221 & 222). "Cycle" them forward and backward, moving one or both legs at a time.

Feet—Rotating, Outer Edge, Inner Edge, Pulling Up, Stretching

Since manually stimulating the Achilles tendon is impossible when sitting on a horse (see p. 81 for how to do it on the ground), the following exercises are indispensable. Some of them can be done with your feet either in or out of the stirrups:

▸ Rotate the tip of your foot in both directions (photo 223).
▸ Tilt your foot onto its outer edge.
▸ Tilt your foot onto its inner edge (photo 224).
▸ Bend and stretch your toes.
▸ Repeat on both sides.

"Monkey Pose"

Be sure to include some time in "monkey pose" to integrate all joints. For a detailed description of how to use "monkey pose" in the saddle, see p. 172.

For a detailed description of how to use "monkey pose" in the saddle, see p. 172.

POINT 6:

Forward-Driving Aids

As mentioned, working on your cross-coordination is one of the best ways to improve your forward-driving aids in the saddle.

Opposite Movements

Eyes vs. head: Turn your head to the right while turning your eyes to the left, and vice versa (photo 225).

Head vs. shoulders: Turn your head to the right while moving your right shoulder to the left. Repeat in other direction (photo 226).

Shoulders vs. hips: Turn your shoulders and hips in opposite directions (photo 227). You can also do this exercise while letting your shoulders remain passive. Cross your arms in front of your chest and place your hands on your shoulder joints. With the help of your hands, turn your shoulders to the left while moving your left hip to the right, and vice versa.

Outstretched arms vs. head: Stretch out your arms perpendicular to your body and grasp one hand with the other. Turn your head right while moving your outstretched arms to the left, rotating around your midline. Repeat in the opposite direction (photo 228).

Outstretched arms vs. hips: Begin the same way as above, but this time while turning your arms to the right, move your right hip to the left, and vice versa (photo 229).

Twisting in "Monkey Pose"

Shorten your stirrups significantly and assume the "monkey pose" (forward seat). Perform "the twist"—your pelvis rotates opposite your shoulders while your arms and hands (relaxed) follow the motion of your shoulders, crossing your body's midline (photo 230).

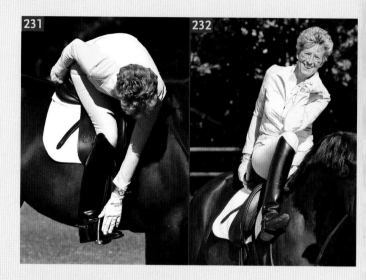

Hand-to-Foot

This exercise depends on oppositional torque (force that produces rotation). While in the saddle, move one arm in the direction of the opposite foot. Have your eyes follow the movement. Alternate from left to right (photo 231). Your hands need to touch the opposite feet several times, crossing your body's midline.

Elbows-to-Knees

Take your feet out of the stirrups and let your legs become heavy while hanging down in a relaxed manner. Lift your right knee up and diagonally toward your left elbow, which moves downward to meet your knee. Repeat with the other elbow and knee across the other diagonal (photo 232).

Inside Leg/Outside Rein

Practice using your inside leg to "push" your horse rhythmically toward your outside rein. Make sure your leg does not pinch or become stiff. Your instructor can place a hand underneath your leg to check direction, amount of strength, and rhythm of your forward-driving movements (see p. 166). This exercise improves your ability to ride on curved lines and to apply diagonal aids.

Resources

Bibliography (Original German Sources)

Andrews, E., Muskel-Coaching. Angewandte Kinesiologie in Sport und Therapie. Freiburg 1993
Ayres, A. J., Bausteine der kindlichen Entwicklung. Die Bedeutung der Integration der Sinne für die Entwicklung des Kindes. Berlin 1998
Beckmann, H., Schöllhorn, W., Differenzielles Lernen im Kugelstoßen. In: Leistungssport 36 (2006) 4
Bauer, A. O., Funktionelle Wirbelsäulengymnastik und Rückentraining. Stuttgart 2007
Bertram, A. M., Laube, W., Sensomotorische Koordination. Gleichgewichtstraining mit dem Kreisel. Stuttgart/New York 2008
Chatzopoulos, D., Die Bedeutung der Aufgabenstellung für Lernprozesse im Sportunterricht. Köln 1997
Christian, P., Vom Wertbewusstsein des Tuns. Ein Beitrag zur Psychomotorik der Willkürbewegung. In: Buytendijk, F. J., Christian, P., Plügge, H., Über die menschliche Bewegung als Einheit von Natur und Geist. Schorndorf 1963
Dennison, G. E., Dennison, P. E., Brain-Gym für Kinder. Kirchzarten 2006 a
Dennison, G. E., Dennison, P. E., Edu-Kinesthetik für Kinder. Handbuch für Edu-Kinethetik. Kirchzarten 2006 b
Dennison, G. E., Dennison, P. E., Brain-Gym Lehrerhandbuch. Kirchzarten 2006 c
Dennison, P. E., Brain-Gym – mein Weg: Lernen mit Lust und Leichtigkeit. Kirchzarten 2006
Egger, K., Lernübertragungen in der Sportpädagogik. Basel 1975
Ennenbach, W., Bild und Mitbewegung. Köln 1989
Feldenkrais, M., Bewusstheit durch Bewegung. Der aufrechte Gang. Frankfurt a. M. 2008
Feldenkrais, M., Die Feldenkraismethode in Aktion. Paderborn 2006
Gallwey, W. T., Tennis, das innere Spiel. München 1991
Goddard, S., Greifen und Be-Greifen. Kirchzarten bei Freiburg 2000, 2. Auflage
Göhner, U., Bewegungslehre im Sport. Schorndorf 1987, 2. Aufl.
Göhner, U., Einführung in die Bewegungslehre. Band 1. Reinbek 1992
Göhner, U., Einführung in die Bewegungslehre. Band 2. Reinbek 1999
Groeben, B., Wolters, P., Bewegungsanweisungen – Hilfe oder Hindernis? In: Laging, R., Prohl, R. (Hg.), Bewegungskompetenz als Bildungsdimension. Hamburg 2005
Hannaford, C., Bewegung – das Tor zum Lernen. Kirchzarten bei Freiburg 2008, 7. Auflage
Hirtz, P., Hotz, O., Ludewig, G., Bewegungskompetenzen. Gleichgewicht. Schorndorf 2000
Hirtz, P., Hotz, O., Ludewig, G., Bewegungskompetenzen. Bewegungsgefühl. Schorndorf 2003
Hirtz, P., Nüske, F. (Hg.), Bewegungskoordination und sportliche Leistung integrativ betrachtet. Hamburg 1997
Kassat, G., Ereignis Bewegungslernen. Rödingshausen 1998
Kirchner, G., Pöhlmann, R., Lehrbuch der Sportmotorik. Kassel 2005
Klingelhöffer, W., Kinesiologie im Sport. Strategie für den Erfolg. Penzberg 2005
Leist, K.-H., Transfer im Sport. Schorndorf 1978
Leist, K.-H., Loibl, J., Vom gefühlvollen Sich-Bewegen und seiner Vermittlung. In: Leist, K. H., Lernfeld Sport: Perspektiven einer Bewegungskultur. Reinbek 1993
Leist, K.-H., Bewegungslernen und Transfer. In: Moegling, K. (Hg.), Integrative Bewegungslehre. Teil III. Immenhausen bei Kassel 2002
Loosch, E., Allgemeine Bewegungslehre. Wiebelsheim 1999
Kolb, M., Methodische Prinzipien zur Entwicklung der Körperwahrnehmung. In: Schierz, M., Hummel, A., Balz, E. (Hg.), Sportpädagogik. Orientierungen, Leitideen, Konzepte. St. Augustin 1994

Meinel, K., Schnabel, G., Bewegungslehre – Sportmotorik. Aachen 2007

Meyners, E., Reiten und Wahrnehmen – eine notwendige Beziehung zur Entwicklung des Bewegungsgefühls. In: FN (Hg.) Dokumentation der 2. Schulsporttagung 1998. Warendorf 1999

Meyners, E., Spielen und Wahrnehmen. Vortrag vor Niedersachsens Sportseminarleitern. In: Turnen und Sport 73 (1999)

Meyners, E., Bewegung in der Schule am Menschen und nicht primär am kulturell geprägten Sport orientieren. In: Paulus, P., Brückner, G. (Hg.), Wege zu einer gesünderen Schule. Tübingen 2000

Meyners, E., Das Bewegungsgefühl des Reiters. Stuttgart 2003

Meyners, E., Das 6-Punkte-Programm für besseres Reiten. Teil 1. In: Reiter Revue (2005) 2, (inkl. DVD). Teil 2: Die richtigen Muskeln zum effektiven Treiben. In: Reiter Revue (2005) 3

Meyners, E., Das Bewegungsgefühl im Reiten. In: Brückner, S. (Hg.), Hippo-logisch? Interdisziplinäre Beiträge namhafter Hippologen rund um das Thema Pferd. Warendorf 2005 a

Meyners, E., Wohlbefinden im Alltag und Arbeitsleben. Stuttgart 2005 b

Meyners, E., Bewegungsgefühl und Reitersitz. Stuttgart 2005 c

Meyners, E., Aufwärmprogramm für Reiter. Stuttgart 2008 a

Meyners, E., Balance und Harmonie des Reiters. In: Dressurstudien 2008 b

Nitsch, J. R., Neumaier, A., Oliver, N., Zur Fertigkeitsspezifik der Gleichgewichtsregulation. In: Loosch, E., Tamme, M. (Hg.), Motorik – Struktur und Funktion. Hamburg 1997

Nitsch, J. R., Neumaier, A., Mester, J., de Marées, H., Techniktraining – Beiträge zu einem interdisziplinären Ansatz. Hofmann 1997

Nitsch, J. R., Sportliches Handeln als Handlungsmodell. In: Sportwissenschaft 5 (1997) 1

Schöllhorn, W., Individualität – ein vernachlässigter Parameter? In: Leistungssport 29 (1999) 2

Schöllhorn, W., Eine Sprint- und Laufschule. Aachen 2003

Schöllhorn, W., Sechelmann, M., Trockel, M., Westers, R., Nie das Richtige trainieren, um richtig zu lernen. In: Leistungssport 34 (2004) 5

Schöllhorn, W., Differenzielles Lehren und Lernen von Bewegung – Durch veränderte Annahmen zu neuen Konsequenzen. In: Gabler, H., Göhner, U., Schiebl, F. (Hg.), Zur Vernetzung von Forschung und Lehre in Biomechanik, Sportmotorik und Trainingswissenschaft. Hamburg 2005

Schöllhorn, W., Michelbrink, M., Grzybowsky, C., Gleichgewichtstraining. DVD. Weikersheim 2007

Schöllhorn, W., Schnelligkeitstraining. DVD. Weikersheim 2006

Schöllhorn, W., Humpert, V. u. a., Differenzielles und Mentales Training im Tennis. In: Leistungssport 38 (2008) 6

Sterr, C., Mentaltraining im Sport. Bessere Leistung bei Training und Wettkampf. Hamburg 2006, 2. Aufl.

Teplitz, J. V., Brain-Gym fürs Büro. Freiburg 2004

Trebels, A.H., Bewegungsgefühl: Der Zusammenhang von Spüren und Bewirken. In: Zeitschrift für Sportpädagogik 14 (1990)

Volger, B., Lehren von Bewegungen. Ahrensburg 1990

Weineck, J., Optimales Training. Erlangen 2007, 15. Aufl.

Weizsäcker, V. v., Der Gestaltkreis – Theorie der Einheit von Wahrnehmen und Bewegen. Stuttgart 1986. 5. Aufl.

Wolters, P., Bewegung unterrichten. Hamburg 2006

Index